British Science and Politics since 1945

Tom Wilkie

BLACKWELL
Oxford UK & Cambridge USA

First published 1991

Basil Blackwell Ltd
109 Cowley Road, Oxford, OX4 1JF, UK

Basil Blackwell, Inc.
3 Cambridge Center
Cambridge, Massachusetts 02142, USA

British Library Cataloguing in Publication Data

A CIP catalogue record for this book is available from the British Library.

Library of Congress Cataloging in Publication Data

Wilkie, Tom.
    British science and politics since 1945 / Thomas Wilkie.
      p. cm. − (Making contemporary Britain)
    Includes index.
    ISBN 0−631−16849−4   ISBN 0−631−16851−6 (pbk.)
    1. Science − Great Britain − History − 20th century.   I. Title.
II. Series.
Q127.G4W62 1991
509′.41′09045 − dc20   90−27560
                                                          CIP

Typeset in 11 on 13 pt Ehrhardt
by Setrite Typesetters Ltd.
Printed in Great Britain by Billings and Sons Ltd

British Science and Politics since 1945

Steve Sly

Wellcome Unit for the
History of Medicine
Manchester University
May 1994

Making Contemporary Britain

General Editor: Anthony Seldon
Consultant Editor: Peter Hennessy

Institute of Contemporary British History
34 Tavistock Square, London WC1H 9EZ

Contents

General Editor's Preface

The Institute of Contemporary British History's series *Making Contemporary Britain* is aimed directly at students in schools and universities and at others interested in learning more about topics in post-war British history. In the series, authors are less attempting to break new ground than presenting clear and balanced overviews of the state of knowledge on each of the topics.

The ICBH was founded in October 1986 with the objective of promoting the study of British history since 1945 at every level. To that end, it publishes books and a quarterly journal, *Contemporary Record*; it organizes seminars and conferences for school students, undergraduates, researchers and teachers of post-war history; and it runs a number of research programmes and other activities.

A central theme of the ICBH's work is that post-war history is too often neglected in British schools, institutes of higher education and beyond. The ICBH acknowledges the validity of the arguments against the study of recent history, notably the problems of bias, of overly subjective teaching and writing, and the difficulties of perspective. But it believes that the values of studying post-war history outweigh the drawbacks, and that the health and future of a liberal democracy require that its citizens know more about the most recent past of their country than the limited knowledge possessed by British citizens, young and old, today. Indeed, the ICBH believes that the dangers of political indoctrination are higher where the young are not informed of the recent past.

The pace of scientific and technological change in Britain has been intense. Its impact has been ubiquitous, affecting the food we eat, the products we buy, the way we travel, our working environment, our health and much else. The story is rich in fascination, and is intimately connected with the progress, or lack of it, of the British economy. One might have expected, therefore, a mass of literature on the history of British science and technology since the war, yet the shelves are almost bare.

Tom Wilkie's concise and well-informed book is thus a major breakthrough in which he brings together many strands. Modestly describing himself as 'merely a journalist', the author has written an important work of history on a neglected area, which should be read by all who want to gain a balanced understanding of post-war British history.

Anthony Seldon

Preface and Acknowledgements

I am not a historian, but a journalist who started out life as a physicist. To most journalists, history is what was in the first edition of the paper; and the business of most scientists is prediction, not the past. I am therefore doubly disqualified from writing history, and this book is not intended as an academic account of the period, but as an overview that points out some of the major landmarks now being gradually shrouded as the mists of time descend. There is no difficult technical or scientific language in the book, and I hope that the narrative will catch and retain the interest of the general reader who wants to follow the tale of one fundamental component of modern society. It might also, I hope, appeal as an introduction to the period for students starting out on the study of science history. It should certainly demonstrate to them how much more there is to find out and to write about.

I would like to thank Sir David Phillips, Chairman of the Advisory Board for the Research Councils, and Dr David Edgerton, of Manchester University, for reading a draft of this book. Although many changes have been made as a result of their comments, the errors of omission and commission that may remain are, of course, my own. I would also like to thank my wife for treating me rather like an ageing motorbike and providing the occasional kick-start necessary to get the book written and completed.

Tom Wilkie

1 Introduction

Every scientist's proper concern is with the future. On a technical level, most of science is about performing experiments and predicting their outcome; but science also operates at a different level where its influence spreads far beyond the confines of the laboratory to shape society's future. Yesterday's chlorofluorocarbon (CFC) refrigerant gas is today's destroyer of the ozone layer; today's recherché experiment on the expression of DNA in mammalian cells may be tomorrow's cure for AIDS.

Perhaps because of their professional focus on the future, scientists tend to have little sense of history. No physicists learning their trade today would think of consulting, say, Einstein's original publications on the theory of relativity, even though relativity is still one of the cornerstones of a physicist's education. It seems almost perverse that, until comparatively recently, many historians of science have tended to focus on the development of scientific concepts and have struggled to write about science as a history of ideas. It is hard for an outsider to see the point of writing such history. One could as fruitfully write a history of art which describes the Sistine Chapel but omits to mention Michelangelo. In other fields, such as political or economic history, the account and analysis of past events is interesting in its own right, but it has a further value because a fuller understanding of the past may provide a springboard to future action. It is not so with the history of science. No one struggling today to produce a fully renormalizable quantum field theory of strong and electroweak nuclear interactions is going to be helped in their quest by reading about, say, the development of the concept of inertia in pre-Newtonian dynamics.

There is history to be written: not so much of science considered as an abstract body of ideas, but rather of the scientists, of the institutions where they worked, of their pay-masters, of those who commissioned and those who benefited from their research. The twentieth century has seen vast changes in science, the way in which it is done, and the way in which it is financed. These developments have paralleled changes of equal moment in society itself, brought about in no small measure by the organization of science on a grand scale and its application to practical ends. Since the end of the Second World War, the pace of technological change has quickened and continues to accelerate. The state has become and continues to be one of the principal paymasters of science.

In Britain, for most of the post-war period, science was perceived as the engine of progress, as the driving force for industrial innovation and economic prosperity, as the principal route to conquering disease, and the only sure hope for better-ment of the human condition. Matters are very different today. There is the scent of a sea change in the air. British scientists have been extraordinarily creative and productive in ideas and experiments in 'pure' science. Yet in recent years, morale has sunk low and few young British scientists are taking the plane to Stockholm to collect a Nobel Prize, the international mark of merit in the basic sciences. Why, having ridden the crest of the wave for so long, should Britain's scientists find that the tide is no longer flowing their way? The British are not in-herently more clever than the French or the Italians or the Germans, so any route to understanding the country's past productivity must start by examining the institutions and struc-tures that existed to foster such creativity, and how they have changed over the years.

There is also a common perception that whereas the British may have been clever at basic science, they have proved less talented at securing practical benefit from that creativity. This has been a constant preoccupation of governments since the end of the war. Here, too, attitudes have changed in recent years, and government has retreated from its previously active role in sponsoring research applicable to private industry.

Surprisingly little has been written about the recent history of science and technology in Britain or about the relationship between science and the state since the end of the war. It is not an empty truism to remark that the war ended a long time ago. More than a professional lifetime now separates us from the events of those days. Young men and women who were just finishing their degree courses to embark upon the enterprise of science at the start of the post-war era are now enjoying quiet retirement. Young people starting out to study science today do not just come to a new world of scientific ideas compared to that earlier generation, but must also find their way round the new institutions and organizations that have come into being over the past half-century.

The period is too short, and the 1940s are still too close, for it to be sensible to attempt an intellectual history of science. In some sciences, molecular biology for example, the important ideas fell into place at the beginning of the post-war period and the history of the subject has been the story of the working out of the implications of these ideas: the paradigm within which the majority of practitioners have worked was established early. Other sciences, subnuclear physics for example, have not found a synthesis and the task of the theoreticians has been that of model-makers while the history of the period is strewn with rejected models, making it more difficult to pick out the events of significance. One feature of the period has been that institutions wax and wane faster than ideas within the sciences that they serve. It is possible to trace the development of the research council system that exists today to support scientists pursuing curiosity-driven research; it is possible also to track the rise and abrupt fall in the political prestige that science has enjoyed over the past half-century or so. These matters are the subject of this book.

In the main, I have concentrated on the relations between government and science, partly because the role of the state as sponsor of science has undergone tremendous changes in the post-war period, and partly also because the documentation is clearer and it is easier to trace what has gone on.

The first point to note is that there is really no such thing as 'science': there are different sciences which at best share a common methodology, but their subject matter and vocabulary have little in common with each other. Moreover, even within one scientific discipline, research can be performed for very different purposes. Such distinctions have often been overlooked in discussions of science policy since the end of the war. Chapter 2 attempts to disaggregate science and clarify the subject matter of the rest of the book.

One of the characteristics of the post-war period up to about 1970 was the remarkable consistency of government policy towards science. As chapter 3 discusses, the prevalent attitude and policy of those times had deep historical roots stretching back to the First World War. The dominant theme of the initial post-war period, as outlined in chapter 4, was the very rapid growth in manpower and money devoted to science in Britain and the *ad hoc* growth of new bodies, such as the Atomic Energy Authority, to disburse government funds. Then, in the space of just a few years, between 1964 and 1971, there was a revolution that utterly disrupted the consensus which had guided science policy for the previous half-century. Indeed, as described in chapter 5, there was not one but two revolutions. The story of Mrs Thatcher's decade (chapter 6) has been in no small measure the working out of the revolution of the early 1970s, but with the added complication of the government's wish to apply the discipline of the marketplace to science as to other areas of national life. A summary and conclusions are presented in chapter 7.

One of the principal omissions from this book is the role of military, or defence, science. Here my excuse is simply that there is not enough information in the public domain to construct any sort of coherent narrative. A lifetime's unremitting labour might perhaps achieve something, but even then it seems to me that the pay-off would be uncertain. The most important defence science programmes since the war are those connected with nuclear weapons and it is unlikely that enough hard information about this topic will be released into the Public Record Office for decades to come.

The book does not concentrate solely on academic science, but also traces some of the attempts that have been made to harness science to practical ends, such as assisting industrial innovation and economic growth. A number of larger companies have begun to commission official histories in which there are accounts of some of the work of their research laboratories, but a detailed account of the history of scientists in industry has still to be written. There is space in this book only to scratch the surface.

2 What is Science?: Why and How the State Invests in Science

The quarter-century from 1928 to 1953 was a period of scientific creativity unparalleled since Galileo and Newton began modern science three centuries before. In 1928, the German physicist Werner Heisenberg and the British theorist Paul Dirac finally solved the puzzle of quantum mechanics and put twentieth-century science on a firm foundation. The period closed with the much-publicized discovery by Watson and Crick of the double helix structure of DNA, the molecule that carries the genetic blueprint for life itself. On the way were such developments as penicillin, radar, the transistor, atomic energy and the atomic bomb. With the exception of penicillin, none of these innovations could have been made without the prior work that went into the development of quantum mechanics. But, without exception, these developments arose from 'organized' science paid for either by the state or by large commercial companies enjoying a secure and almost monopolistic position in the marketplace.

The Second World War was the physicists' war just as the Great War had been the chemists', and the experience confirmed the lesson taught by the First World War: that no modern state could hope to survive without organizing science and harnessing its power to political ends. In the judgement of the Oxford historian of science, Margaret Gowing, 'The second world war was scientific from top to bottom: from major new science-based weapon systems that might dominate strategy and the outcome of the war, to, in beleaguered Britain, the nutrition of the whole population, whether munitions workers or expectant mothers.[1] Of all the triumphs of science, however, none so impressed governments as the Manhattan Project, through which the USA obtained the atomic bomb. Here, for all to see, was the promise and the power of science when deployed for the purposes of the state.

The war accelerated many scientific and technological developments, but it also marked a change in the style of science. The age had long since passed when a gifted individual — a Newton or a James Prescott Joule — could work successfully alone or in correspondence with other members of a learned academy. But the war marked the passing of the second era of modern science: the era of the great university laboratories, begun in Germany in the 1820s and reaching an apotheosis in the 1930s with Rutherford's Cavendish Laboratory at Cambridge. A new age had begun[2] and with it the inexorable rise of 'big science'. The Manhattan Project itself and within it, the Los Alamos Laboratory, were the forerunners of a new style of, and a new form of organization for, doing science. None the less, that the war marked a great watershed within science itself was hardly perceived at the time: nearly 20 years were to elapse before the phrase 'big science' was actually coined.[3] Throughout most of the post-war period, British scientists were busy bringing their subject out of the Age of Academies by setting up or expanding laboratories and research schools in the style of the Cavendish, without fully realizing that history was already moving on.

Science has two aspects: it is a cultural activity, and it is an activity with immense practical application. To investigate the fundamental constituents of the material world — the domain of elementary particle physics — or our relationship as animals to the rest of the living world and the nature of life itself — the realms of the evolutionary and molecular biologists — are activities just as 'cultural' as music or the theatre, which governments support as a matter of course. In the early years of this century following the discovery of the electron, Jacob Bronowski remarked, physics had become 'the greatest collective work of science — no, more than that, the great collective work of art in the twentieth century'.[4] It is also notable that science is a distinctive product of the Western cultural tradition: music and the performing arts are all but universal, science is a rare and unusual creation.

Science would scarcely receive support to the extent that it does if governments did not hope also for practical application. Science is not just a way of investigating the world, it also opens the door to changing it. Physicists have found a way of releasing thermonuclear energy — hitherto unknown on the face of the earth, but confined in nature to the centres of the stars themselves in the remote fastnesses of space — while biologists have created new creatures that could not have come about by the normal processes of sexual reproduction and evolution by natural selection. The result of the physicists' researches was the hydrogen bomb, which has dominated international politics in our time; the creatures created by the biologists have been given valuable characteristics, such as the ability to manufacture pharmaceutical drugs as part of their inherent physiology, which will transform the health of nations in the future.

In 1971, Lord Dainton, the distinguished chemist and public servant, summarized this dual nature of science and the rationale for government to support the scientific enterprise:

> Science is a means of obtaining knowledge about the structure and characteristics of the animate and inanimate world, and its importance to human society is that such knowledge lies at the base of nearly all human activities that influence positively or negatively the quality of human life and its environment. Science makes major contributions to the improvement of health; to the provision of good food, shelter, transport and communication; to the efficient use and conservation of natural resources and the maintenance of a good physical environment; to education; and to the development and maintenance of an internationally competitive industry leading to a healthy economy. It is because Governments are aware of the power of science to serve national goals that they are prepared to provide substantial national resources to sustain scientific activities over and above those

which any civilised society must allow responsive and creative individuals to advance knowledge in any sphere.[5]

The far-reaching implications of scientific research pose serious problems for its industrial and political paymasters. How are they to identify those areas of science which should be supported as part of a civilized society allowing creative individuals to advance knowledge? How are they to tell those areas of science that will help improve the industrial economy and the quality of human life? Sometimes, it is easy: the significance of the invention of the transistor was immediately apparent: that it would revolutionize electronics and tele-communications was clear, although no one in the late 1940s could have imagined the extent of that revolution or predicted that the transistor's progeny, the integrated circuit or microchip, would lead amongst many other things to the development of immensely powerful personal computers such as the one on which this book was written. Sometimes it is not so easy. When lasers were developed in the late 1950s and early 1960s, few of the applications immediately foreseen subsequently materialized and for a time they seemed laboratory curiosities. No one then could have predicted that within 30 years one of their principal applications would be a commonplace domestic item, the core component of compact disc players. Nor is the past any guide to the future: research into atomic and nuclear physics in the 1920s and 1930s led directly to the atom bomb and to nuclear energy, so this line of work was continued after the war, yet it has yielded little of practical application; even a project deliber-ately intended to have practical effect − the attempt to control thermonuclear fusion as a source of power − has proved unsuccessful.

The struggle to distinguish in advance the areas of science that will have fruitful consequences in the realm of practical affairs from those that are concerned solely with the advancement of knowledge has spawned a lexicon of its own. The classifi-cations have included 'pure' as opposed to 'applied' science; through 'applicable' and 'exploitable'; to 'basic' as opposed to 'strategic' research. However, in 1981, the OECD did manage to agree clear standard definitions of 'basic research'; 'applied research' and 'experimental development'.[6] These are discussed in an Appendix to this book. The British government for its own reasons seems to feel that the definitions are inadequate and has added more terms, including 'strategic' and 'near-market' research.[7]

The problem is not just one of intellectual or linguistic curiosity; it is of vital economic and commercial importance. Scientific research and development is costly. It requires very highly educated and therefore expensive manpower, and increasingly it requires expensive equipment and facilities. Moreover, it is costly in terms of time as well as money: in the pure science of radioastronomy, for example, the discovery of pulsars in 1967 led to the award of a Nobel Prize to the Cambridge astronomers Martin Ryle and Anthony Hewish, but the essential foundations for the discovery had lain in the basic research which they had led at Cambridge for two decades since the end of the Second World War. In industrial research, more than a decade elapsed between the development of the transistor and its large-scale incorporation into commercially available computers. Even commercial companies that have the financial resources to fund in-house research and development may balk at the lead-times involved, or may find that a competitor has come earlier to the marketplace perhaps with an inferior product but by getting there first establishes an advantage that the later, superior product is unable to overcome. The adoption of the VHS system of domestic video recorders as a *de facto* world standard, rather than the Betamax system, is a nice example of the marketplace opting for a product which is not the best technically (although it is not obvious in this case that there were deficiencies in research and development programmes that influenced the final outcome).

There is a further complication in classifying scientific research and hence deciding who is to pay for it. The product of a piece of scientific research is in some sense 'intellectual property', either a refinement to a human invention or an addition to our stock of knowledge about the natural world. The property is expensive to acquire, but not all research is equally valuable in a commercial sense. Some results of research can be protected, by patents and other forms of intellectual property rights, so that the researcher or his employer can benefit and obtain a return on the investment put into the research in the first place. But there are other scientific discoveries that cannot be so protected. The law of gravity, for example, is not patentable. Indeed, the result of much scientific research is publicly available as papers published in the open literature in scientific journals. The fruits of this type of research, usually called pure or academic or basic science, are what the economists term a public good — they cannot be appropriated exclusively by any individual or group for private purposes. But although this type of science may be a public good it is not a free good; it is rather expensive to acquire such knowledge. No commercial company will consider that it benefits from paying for the type of research whose outcome is a public good, for such a strategy would mean expending the shareholders' money to obtain a product that would equally benefit the company's competitors and who would have acquired a competitive advantage because they obtained this new knowledge without having had to pay for it.

There is thus a natural dichotomy among the paymasters of science. Large commercial companies will fund their own research programmes, where the research will be directed to specific applications improving either the company's products or the process by which they are made, and the company's managers will be diligent to ensure that the fruits of the creativity of their research laboratories are fully protected as the company's intellectual property. But this type of research is inescapably founded on the pre-existing knowledge base about the natural world: there must already be a stock of knowledge publicly available and ready for development and then application by the company's scientists. Since the company itself is not willing to pay for such knowledge, it has become natural for governments to fund the 'pure' or 'academic' science which can then be developed and exploited for economic gain by private companies. For example, no mining company is going to undertake the task of mapping the geology of the whole of Britain; such an operation has fallen naturally to the government-funded British Geological Survey, set up in the nineteenth century for precisely this purpose. Mining companies may use the maps as indicators of the likely locations of mineral deposits. A company can then undertake its own applied research focused on the specific region it thinks most likely to contain an exploitable deposit. The maps produced by the British Geological Survey are therefore an example of 'the power of science to serve national goals' for which governments are prepared to provide substantial national resources. But laying the foundations for the better development of the national economy is not the only outcome of the Survey's work. The advancement of knowledge has been served too, by the increase in the proper understanding of the geology of the country that has come about as a result of the Survey's activities. (Since the Survey's establishment in the nineteenth century, most of the country has been mapped and there is currently a questionmark over its future. A final decision has yet to be taken over its status and the arrangements for its continued funding.)

There is a further element to the state's involvement. The research that is done in company laboratories requires manpower trained to the highest standards and it is in general unreasonable to suppose that a commercial organization already committed to expensive applied research and development would also undertake the training of its own researchers. Thus the government-funded laboratories in the universities and research institutes have a dual function, not only do they provide the knowledge base, they are also the establishments in which the manpower, necessary for private industry's research pro-grammes, is trained. It is arguable that, of the two functions, training in research methods is possibly the more important.

It will be apparent from the preceding discussion that although the boundary may be clear, in principle, between research that is a public good and that which is private property, in practice the demarcation is fuzzy. As the example of the work of the Geological Survey shows, there is but the finest of lines between pure research (a better understanding of the country's geology) and applied research (the likely locations of profitable mineral deposits). The role of the state is complicated because it is not just the provider of public scientific knowledge, but also the educator of scientists both for the public domain of university or government laboratories and for the private domain of industrial research and development.

Even this picture is an oversimplification. On occasions, the state has decided that it should itself become the producer of high-technology goods, and therefore governments have found it necessary to establish large teams of research scientists and development engineers to perform the necessary preliminary work. The most obvious examples in the post-war period are nuclear power, both civil and military, and the procurement of military equipment, aircraft particularly. A second area of state intervention has stemmed from a continuing perception that British industry is not investing enough of its own resources in the sort of science and engineering that will lead to innovative and valuable products competitive on the world market. It has therefore seemed logical for many governments to subsidize some of industry's own research and development costs, to carry out quasi-industrial research in state-financed laboratories, to use procurement contracts as a means of stimulating research, or to try to coordinate the disparate research of several companies into a coherent programme covering a complete industrial sector.

Even within government itself, science is done for a variety of purposes and this is reflected in the different ways in which it is financed. Most individual departments of state have, as part of their annual allocation from the Treasury, funds earmarked to be spent on scientific research. In general, this will be 'applied' research but the work will be applied to the purposes of government and not, in general, directed to innovation from which the country as a whole or some specific company is likely to derive economic benefit. One example was the decision of the Ministry of Agriculture, Fisheries and Food (MAFF) early in 1990 to spend some £6 million over three years on research into bovine spongiform encephalopathy (BSE), known more colloquially as 'mad cow disease'. Clearly it was relevant to MAFF's statutory roles relating to animal health and to the safety of food for human consumption for the Ministry to find out how extensive this disease was and how easy or difficult would be its transmission from already infected to previously undiseased cattle and the likelihood of its transmission to humans and other species. In addition to the public and animal health aspects, better knowledge of the disease would be likely to aid the farming industry financially both in domestic markets and in other countries of the European Community, who have prohibited the import of certain categories of beef products from the UK to prevent the disease spreading to them. Historically, MAFF has often regarded itself as a sponsoring department for the agricultural industry, and so would naturally undertake such work for the indirect financial benefit of producers. It was not part of the MAFF programme of research to study the causative agent (which is as yet unknown) and that work is being funded separately.

A second example of research relevant to a department's administrative function is the work funded by the Department of the Environment into radioactive waste disposal. At an annual cost of about £11 million, this is the department's largest single research programme relating to environmental protection. The department is not trying to find sites that would be suitable for waste disposal – that is the function of the geologists and other scientists working for UK Nirex, the nuclear industry's waste disposal company – but among other things it does need to acquire the information and techniques necessary for HM Inspectorate of Pollution to discharge its statutory responsibilities to assess and regulate what the nuclear industry might propose, and to be able independently of the industry to perform risk assessment studies.

Research intended to assist departments discharge their administrative functions, whether regulatory or policy-making, is generally 'applied' research, and it may be performed extra-murally by some agency under contract to deliver a specific piece of research or intra-murally within the department's own laboratories under the direction of the department's chief scientist. The mechanism by which the government funds basic science, the research whose outcome leads to a public good, is quite different. This research is funded through a block grant from the Department of Education and Science to five statutory research councils, who then decide how the money is to be divided up and which scientists and scientific projects are to be supported. In addition, scientists working in universities are supported by the Department of Education and Science through another route: the Department also gives a block grant to the University Grants Committee (now the Universities Funding Council), which pays researchers' salaries and for the upkeep of buildings. Thus, for example, the causative agent of BSE and the detailed physiological effects of the disease are being studied by scientists funded by one of the research councils, the Agricultural and Food Research Council, in a programme that is financially quite separate from that of MAFF mentioned earlier. However, there is no clear demarcation of applied and pure science within the government structure: in addition to this 'pure' work on BSE, the Agricultural and Food Research Council also holds contracts to carry out some of the applied research on BSE that MAFF is funding.

It will be apparent that 'science' is a portmanteau word for a series of diverse activities, carried out for a variety of purposes. Industry's needs are comparatively straightforward: it applies scientific knowledge to reap commercial gain (although to a lesser extent it may also need to conduct scientific research to ensure that it is complying with government or other regulations). In a few arenas, the state too applies science in the expectation of an economic return. It has established a large technical expertise in the defence field, where it is the primary purchaser. The state also needs science to support the administrative and policy functions of government while it funds basic research for the public good and trains the next generation of researchers. But the state has historically also funded applied commercial research whose ultimate outcome was not intended to be a public good but private gain by industrial companies. Thus, there is a complex structure of institutions through which the government channels its support for science, and there is no single rationale for spending money on science: many national goals require some scientific input.

British taxpayers currently spend just under £5 billion on scientific research and development, directly employing some 50,000 people.[8] For comparison, British industry spent just over £4.3 billion of its own money on research and development in 1987, the most recent year for which accurate figures are available. Industry employed 184,000 staff on R&D of whom about 87,000 were professional scientists or engineers. It is worth noting in passing that British industry actually carried out more research than the above figure implies. It financed only about 68 per cent of the R&D work that it performed. The government, out of its total £5 billion, spent some £1.2 billion of the taxpayers' money on research and development in British industry. Additionally, overseas companies commissioned research worth £0.78 billion from British industry.

Nearly half of the government's expenditure is on military research and development (and, one suspects, much of the expenditure under the 'defence R&D' heading is actually closer to procurement than research or even development). Despite the importance of the topic, the all-pervasive secrecy that shrouds Whitehall affairs makes it all but impossible to study defence R&D properly. On civil research and development, the government spends just under £2.5 billion, around 0.58 per cent of the country's gross domestic product in 1988, directly employing around 33,000 staff of whom roughly 12,000 are graduates. (These figures incude an estimate for the staff of the UK Atomic Energy Authority which, although it is financed directly by government and is the largest single R&D organization in Europe, is now perversely left out of the official statistics on government-funded research and development.)[9]

Most of this money is spent directly by the individual departments of state which commission such research as they feel is necessary to guide or support their main tasks of administration. In 1990–1, £897 million of the civil R&D spending was channelled through five research councils to support researchers and research students working in the universities and in the councils' own institutes. Most, but not all, of this research is basic, curiosity-driven science. The Universities Funding Council estimates that, of the money that it distributed to universities in that year, a similar sum, around £800 million, went to the support of academic scientists employed by the universities. Britain does not have a central Ministry of Science and Technology Research, as exists for example in the Federal Republic of Germany, to oversee this expenditure. There is only the weakest of central coordination, by a small unit attached to the Cabinet Office. How this fragmented system grew up and how it has facilitated the devaluation of state-supported civil science, both basic and applied, in the latter part of the post-war period will be one of the main subjects of following chapters.

The fundamental question then when one approaches a history of British science is 'which science?'. In practice, it is not easy to disentangle who is doing what science for what end. Quite often a single research establishment may be carrying out contract research for both industry and government as well as conducting its own programme of basic research.

A central theme of the post-war period, a theme repeated by government and by independent commentators alike, has been that there is a necessary connection between science, innovation and economic development. Even the basic science that the state supported as a matter of the common good was held not just to be a cultural activity performed by Lord Dainton's 'responsive and creative individuals' but also as adding to a stock of knowledge that could be exploited for economic gain. Under this model, the basic scientists made the bricks which the industrial scientists took away to assemble in proper order to build the house. Throughout the post-war period, therefore, there has been a constant blurring of the definitions of science or at least of perceptions of the purpose for which science is done. The story of the government's relationship to the science that it funds has therefore been a series of different answers to the basic question 'What is science for?'. As will become clear, no government has succeeded in answering this question satisfactorily. The history of government policy towards British science is a story of successive re-inventions of the wheel — except that each time it was re-invented, it acquired a different name.

Notes

1 Margaret Gowing, 'The history of science, politics, and political economy', in *Information Sources in the History of Science and Medicine*, ed. Pietro Corsi and Paul Weindling (Butterworths, 1983).

2 Richard G. Hewlett and Oscar E. Anderson jnr, *The New World*, vol. 1 of the official history of the US Atomic Energy Commission (Pennsylvania State University Press, 1962)

3 Derek De Solla Price, *Little Science, Big Science* (Columbia University Press, 1963).

4 Jacob Bronowski, *The Ascent of Man* (BBC, 1973), p. 330.

5 The Future of the Research Council System (The Dainton Report), White Paper, Cmnd 4814 (HMSO, 1971).

6 *The Measurement of Scientific and Technical Activities* (The Frascati Manual) (OECD, Paris, 1981).

7 See, for example, Annual Review of Government Funded R&D 1987, Annexe 2, for definitions (HMSO, 1987).

8 Annual Review of Government Funded R&D 1989 (HMSO, 1989).

9 The UKAEA has been set up to operate on a trading fund basis, so its staff are no longer classed as government employees.

3 The Unfulfilled Dream: How the State Learned that It Must Support Science

In the history of the relationship between British governments and science, the post-war period divides fairly neatly into two. The first runs from the end of the war until about 1970. Throughout that time successive governments believed that there was a necessary connection between science and growing national wealth. At the beginning of the period, there were frantic efforts to try to rectify a perceived shortfall in trained scientific manpower and, towards the end near-panic about the 'brain-drain' of this expensively trained expertise to better-paid jobs (and better facilities) in the USA and elsewhere overseas. Throughout this time, however, governments believed that more money spent on science or the administrative effort involved in reshaping the government machinery for the support of science would inevitably bring economic progress and advantage. In Britain around 1960, science and technology seemed the talisman that would, through modernization, solve the problems of relatively slow economic growth and relative economic decline. At the 1964 General Election, science became a main platform and a rallying cry for both political parties, but more especially for the Labour Party with Harold Wilson's celebrated phrase about the 'white heat' of the scientific revolution.[1]

By 1970, disillusion had set in, and the second period was one of reaction. The boundless benefits of science had not materialized. Britain had continued on a course of relative economic decline; governments were being forced to cut back on their expenditure and science, although a comparatively modest charge on the budget, was a relatively painless cut.

In this respect, Mrs Thatcher's government continued a pre-existing trend. She was the first Prime Minister to have trained as a scientist (although she quickly abandoned chemistry to re-train as a tax lawyer). Under her government there has been once again palpable evidence of a renewed brain-drain,[2] but the evidence has been denigrated as special pleading by just another self-interested lobby group; senior civil servants have spoken of 'a scientists' mountain' in the same disparaging terms as the European Community's 'butter mountain';[3] and the proportion of national resources being devoted to scientific research has fallen considerably. Indeed, for the first time in nearly 70 years, the very idea that the state should be sponsoring scientific research is now open to question.

There is little historical analysis of post-war science to provide any guidance on why there should have been such a transition. Science policy was extensively discussed in the 1980s, but without much reference to the historical background.[4] As Gowing observed, the history of science as it has developed as a profession and intellectual discipline in the English-speaking world has been almost inseparable from the philosophy of science: it is primarily internalist and concerned with the evolution of ideas. 'Scientists were too often treated as a race apart and the turmoil of history was lost. Paradoxically, scientists were being submerged in politics in the 1940s and 1950s just as the history of science profession was propagating the idealist version of science and the scientist as essentially internal, pure, objective, uninterested in power.'[5]

A possible explanation for the change of heart about the role of science might begin with the observation that successive governments have tended to see science policy as a proxy for an industrial policy.[6] It has generally been believed that one of the reasons why British companies are uncompetitive is that they have not invested sufficiently in research and development. For decades, therefore, governments have struggled to formulate policies that would encourage industry to conduct more research — by setting up research associations, for example, that would bring together small companies, which could not individually afford to pay for research, to pool their resources; or by the government itself funding a proportion of the research that it thinks, in the national interest, ought to be done in the industrial sector. This 'pump priming' by governments has been going on for more than 70 years now, yet the pump shows as little sign of working by itself today as in 1918.

A second observation may be that non-scientists — and that means most government ministers and their officials — tend to regard science as an abstract body of knowledge, rather than as an activity carried out by people with a specific aptitude, disposition and training. Thus the recurrent refrain has been that British industry needs to apply more science — as if science were in itself some definable tool or process — whereas the true need was for more scientists. In the face of this need, massive cultural inertia has hindered the production of sufficient scientists and engineers with a broad enough education to meet the needs of a modern industrial nation.[7] But this 'shortage' is not expressed on the labour market in terms of high wages being offered for individuals whose skills are perceived to be in short supply; on the contrary, the pay and conditions of scientists working in industry are notoriously poor; the prevalent cultural prejudice has extended to prevent those who are technically educated from being accorded the status and the renumeration they should have received. A third idea that might be considered is the possibility that governments (both civil servants and ministers) and the major financial institutions simply do not have the necessary background to understand the long lead-times and huge up-front expenditures demanded by the complexities of today's high technology, with the result that considerable sums of money may have been spent but seldom in accordance with a coherent long-term strategy.

But it might be more productive to turn the logic round and address the possibility that the lack of investment in research and development is more likely to be an outward symptom of deeper underlying problems within British industry, that the lack of R&D investment is an effect rather than a cause of industry's problems. The approach was tried briefly by the

Ministry of Technology during the Wilson government of the mid-1960s, which intervened heavily in the private sector in an attempt to restructure Britain's manufacturing industry, with mixed results. But to pursue this train of argument would get us caught up in wider questions of the nature of Britain's industrial and economic decline which are beyond both the scope of this book and the competence of its author.[8] What is relevant here is that in recent years the emphasis among policy-makers has been on the perceived failure of science to deliver the goods – rather than on the failure of industry to capitalize on the talents of the nation's scientists and the knowledge they produced – and so the rationale for state support of science has come into question.

In a sense, the wheel has come full circle. During the nineteenth century, British governments saw little need for the state to become involved financially in supporting individuals who wanted to carry out scientific research or in creating institutions which would promote and facilitate scientific research and, of course, there was no suggestion of government intervention in industry.[9] Then, as now, a major foreign power was exploiting new discoveries in science and technology and founding new industries – with the help of its government – on the basis of new technologies. The role which Japan is playing in the late twentieth century was, towards the end of the nineteenth, played by Imperial Germany. Then, as now, some of the ideas and discoveries that the foreign power adopted and exploited had been made in Britain, but the British had not capitalized upon them. The stresses of the First World War revealed these deficiencies with stark clarity and led to a reversal of policy by the British government and to the foundations of the system for the support of science that we know today. But, after a brief flurry of activity during and immediately after the First World War, the impetus lapsed and Britain went through the Second World War with a science system that had scarcely changed in its essentials for 20 years.

If any sense is to be made of developments after 1945, a brief résumé of events long beforehand is necessary. The British research system in the last decade of the twentieth century is, at base, still the product of a series of reactions to the scientific institutions developed in Germany in the early years of the nineteenth century. In a sense, the UK never really caught up with the innovations that not only made Germany pre-eminent in pure science but put it at the forefront of harnessing science to the purposes of productive industry.

The virtual invention of the research university by Justus von Liebig at Giessen in the years after 1824,[10] marks almost as great a transition in the development of science as occurred in the seventeenth century. But whereas the state in Britain had been in the forefront in establishing institutions to conduct 'modern' science in the seventeenth century — the Royal Greenwich Observatory and the Royal Society — neither the state nor the community of scientists themselves properly made the shift from the Age of Academies. In the practical and expensive conduct of experiments in organized university research laboratories and in the systematic training of research workers there, Germany gained and retained the initiative. Britain still produced brilliant individual researchers, such as Joule and Maxwell, but it was not until late in the century with the formation of the Schuster Laboratory at Manchester and the Cavendish at Cambridge that the German example was copied. These laboratories showed what could be done (the history of early twentieth-century British physics is essentially the story of these two laboratories) but such laboratories remained the exception rather than the rule at British universities until the Second World War. Although the great civic universities of the Midlands and the North might have represented a different path to be taken, on the whole the British preferred Cardinal Newman's elegant evocation of an Athenian ideal of a university even though the nineteenth-century German system had rendered it an anachronism before Newman's essay was written.[11]

As noted previously, 'pure' research laboratories have a dual function. They do not just increase our stock of knowledge about the natural world, they are also places of apprenticeship in which young scientists acquire a training in research methods. Inevitably, more researchers are trained than will later be able to succeed their teachers into posts where they can themselves conduct basic scientific research. The majority will leave the academic laboratory for positions in wider society. Thus the academic research laboratory is a vital institution if a society is to develop a 'scientific culture'. The UK failed to establish a sufficient number of them quickly enough.

The German system was much more centralized and susceptible of direct political interference than the one that has developed in the UK — university professors were regarded as civil servants, for example, and the local state governments were represented on the governing bodies of the universities — and it had a tendency to ossification. Despite this, the system had sufficient resilience to survive and prosper not only while the disparate states were welded into the Prussian Imperium, but also through defeat in the First World War and the subsequent economic chaos of the 1920s. Only with the advent of Hitler did the system break down irretrievably. It seems likely that even without the war and the second defeat in 30 years, the damage done in Hitler's first decade would have been irreparable. The case of Germany demonstrates how easily and quickly a century of achievement in science can be destroyed and how slow, if not impossible, the subsequent recovery may be — for, some 45 years after the end of the war, Germany is only now beginning to recover some of its pre-war standing in basic science.[12]

The system that has grown up in Britain in this century for the state support of civil science is, in contrast to that of Germany, diffuse and decentralized. In the case of basic science, the set of institutions developed in Britain for government support has facilitated the independence of the individual researcher even when the gentleman amateur, characteristic of the nineteenth-century British scientist, came to be replaced by the scientist salaried by the state. It was almost consciously an attempt to preserve for the salaried scientist a professional life as free from external direction as that of his predecessor, the gentleman of private means. Unquestionably this system helped encourage the creativity that British scientists have consistently displayed in the pursuit of pure or basic science.[13]

It is self-evident that the people of no one country have a special aptitude for science. So if a country acquires a reputation for being disproportionately creative in science or effective in turning the fruits of scientific research into products that its industry can sell profitably, then the cause must reasonably lie in the institutions that country has developed to educate its young people in science, to encourage them to push back the frontiers of research, and to promote the smooth transition of the results of research from the laboratory bench to the production line and the sales manager's portfolio. Whether Britain's educational system, or the institutions for capitalizing on the results of the excellent basic research, have functioned anything like as well as its basic science is open to question.

The failures of British science in the nineteenth century were not principally in 'pure' science: the application of science to industry was particularly deficient. In his essay on the two cultures, C.P. Snow also identified two revolutions.[14] The first was the industrial revolution, pioneered in Britain. It was predominantly a matter of practical men of affairs improving the products that they made and the processes by which they were made, using essentially the benefits of their own practical experience. But the British, Snow believed, had failed to master the scientific revolution. They were unprepared for the rational application to industry of research that had often been undertaken without immediate thought of practical application. It was, in Snow's words, 'no longer hit and miss, no longer the ideas of odd "inventors"'. Snow did not date the start of the scientific revolution precisely, but one story, that of aniline dyes,[15] will serve to exemplify his thesis.

In Easter 1856, William Perkin, then aged 17, discovered 'mauveine', the first artificial dyestuff and the foundation of the modern chemical industry. But even though Perkin had made his discovery in the Royal College of Chemistry, the British failed properly to capitalize on Perkin's discovery. It was the German dyestuffs and chemical industry that exploited the new technology, amongst other reasons because they had a plentiful supply of research chemists able to adapt and further develop the discovery. Germany's long tradition of state-supported science meant that, unlike their moribund English counterparts, German universities had been turning out PhD level chemists for a couple of decades before Perkin made his discovery, and so German companies had access to the skilled manpower and expertise they needed. In contrast, British companies were dominated by practical men who had little time for research the value of which was not immediately apparent. Perhaps as important, British industry was and remained fragmented: it consisted of numerous small companies which individually had not the resources to compete on world markets (outside the favourable conditions of the Empire) nor to support long-term research and development. And companies in the same sector of British industry were reluctant to pool their resources in financing even what today would be called 'pre-competitive' research. It was a situation in which the government, under the extreme pressure of the First World War, ultimately felt compelled to intervene.

When hostilities broke out, the War Office was shocked to discover that for commodities vital for the war effort — dyes used to colour British army uniforms, ingredients necessary for the army's explosives, the optical glass used in gun-sights, and the magnetos for what motorized transport there was — Britain was largely dependent on Imperial Germany.[16] In the early months of the First World War, the British government was faced with rectifying deficiencies in private industry and in the nation's application of modern scientific knowledge that were the result of decades of neglect. The problems that the government then faced, and the remedies that it chose to apply, have been the dominant themes of industrial and scientific policy ever since.

Hostilities broke out in August. In December, the British government took the radical step of setting up its own company, the British Dyestuffs Corporation, to rectify some of the shortages.[17] The scientists themselves banded together to offer their services in the national emergency, setting up a Committee on the Neglect of Science in May 1916, with Lord Rayleigh in the chair. On 28 July 1915, the government had set up a Committee of the Privy Council on Scientific and Industrial Research.

Eventually this led to the formation, on 1 December 1916, of the Department of Scientific and Industrial Research (DSIR) which reported to Lord Crewe, then Lord President of the Privy Council. The government also set aside a million pounds — a very large sum of money in those days — to allow the DSIR to get down to work. For the next 50 years, the DSIR was to be one of the main instruments by which the state supported civil science and by which the state encouraged British industry to exploit scientific knowledge and convert science into industrial and economic development.

The DSIR had two controlling bodies. Political control was exercised by the Lord President of the Council and by a committee of the Privy Council, consisting after 1929 of ministers of state. The department's scientific policy was determined by an Advisory Council of distinguished scientists (more than half of them Fellows of the Royal Society). The role of the Advisory Council was to judge the potential fruitfulness of proposed research projects submitted to it. The department's administrative staff was tiny: it rose from 11 in 1915 to only 56 in 1963, the year before its abolition.

The armed forces and the service departments had had an interest in scientific research from very early in the 'modern' period of science: the Royal Greenwich Observatory, for example, was established for military purposes and remained a part of the Admiralty until 1964. The Meteorological Office remains part of the Ministry of Defence to this day. But the establishment of the DSIR was an acknowledgement by government that something fundamental had changed: military research could never have produced the diversity of technologically advanced artefacts that, the war revealed, were necessary for modern military operations. At the DSIR's foundation, the government set its face against concentrating all government research into one department. There was to be no single Ministry for Research and Technology, as for example, the Federal Republic of Germany and to a lesser extent France have today. The role of the DSIR was to be that of a coordinator of research. But this inevitably conflicted with the fact that the department was at the same time commissioning research. It thus came to be perceived as a rival by those other departments of state — principally the armed forces — whose own interest in research had been further stimulated by the First World War, and who maintained and increased their interest afterwards. Eventually, other departments of state became major commissioners of research, with more funds at their disposal than the DSIR, and this, coupled with the lack of clarity about the role of the DSIR, was to prove its undoing.

In the only major study of the work of the DSIR, by Ian Varcoe, this conflict is highlighted as one of the main problems with the post-1918 dispensation. In Varcoe's opinion, the established departments of state were aware of and in some cases concerned with the problems with which it was proposed the DSIR should deal.[18] They were interested in research in so far as it affected their broader administrative responsibilities, but their main concerns lay elsewhere. Consequently, insufficient attention was paid to increasing the output of trained research workers from the universities and to promoting research and development in industry. Where research was conducted into industrial problems, basic research was neglected. Other areas of research were ignored because they were not closely related to any existing administrative field. At the same time, the results of research sometimes failed to find application because the departments concerned tended to ignore information that challenged the policy to which they were committed and for the execution of which they were directly responsible.

Within the DSIR, research was to be more than a means to an end. It was to be an object of policy in its own right. For this reason the recommendations of the Advisory Council would have to 'represent the progressive realisation of a considered programme and policy'. However, following the First World War, there was a growth in research done by government departments. The war had triggered research interests by the War Office, Admiralty, Munitions Ministry, Air Ministry. Subjects such as meteorology, medical and agricultural research were more actively investigated.

The DSIR set up Coordinating Boards to dovetail all this research together in the national interest and to ensure civil spin-off (although it was not, of course, so called at that time) from military research and development. But departmental in-fighting and bad relations between the DSIR and industry put paid to this. The DSIR had no executive control over all government research establishments. Its authority was technical not administrative. Inter-service rivalry and the classification of research as secret killed the civil spin-off. In 1927, the policy of Coordinating Boards collapsed and was replaced by informal *ad hoc* assessors or joint committees were set up when new research areas opened. This remained essentially unchanged into the late 1950s. The problem of trying to secure civil spin-off from classified defence R&D projects has also remained essentially unchanged, and unsolved, through into the 1990s. In 1989, the Prime Minister's own Advisory Council on Science and Technology (ACOST) mounted an investigation, headed by Sir Charles Reece, ICI's director of research, into ways of getting military research establishments to contribute more to the development of the civilian economy. The investigation seems to have had little practical effect.[19]

On the civil and industrial side, the DSIR's principal mech-anism for encouraging industry was to set up research associ-ations. These were intended to bring British companies in one sector of industry together jointly to fund research of relevance to that industry. The government took the lead in setting up the research associations, but industry had to match government grants pound for pound. The first steps were taken in 1917, when the department encouraged groups of firms to come together to form research associations by providing five-year grants. In the immediate post-war years, 23 research associations were formed. But, as early as 1923, it had become apparent that they were underfunded and in the following two years, more research associations were wound up than were formed. In 1923, the DSIR distributed £103,000 to the research associ-ations but that had fallen to £54,000 by 1928 when the associ-ations appealed to the Lord President of the Council for more money. They received some respite and, by 1930, were employ-ing about 250 people of graduate status, but then the money fell again, from £80,000 to £66,000 in 1932. By 1940, there were 21 grant-aided research associations — two fewer than there had been in 1923 — with a total income of £480,000.

Commenting on the patchy history of the industrial research associations, Varcoe remarks that 'the development of the research associations suggests that the judgement of Government in 1916 concerning the organisation of research in industry in the post-war period was unsound.'[20]

Although it was the most radical break with the past, the Department of Scientific and Industrial Research was not actually the first vehicle through which government funds were channelled to the support of scientific research.[21] The first tentative steps towards framing the institutions that exist today actually came the year before the outbreak of war, with the establishment in 1913 of the Medical Research Committee (MRC), set up under the terms of the 1911 National Health Insurance Act. The Act stipulated that for everyone insured under the scheme, the Treasury would make available from public funds one extra penny for medical research. At the time this amounted to about £40,000 a year. There being no Ministry of Health then, the organization to deal with research was responsible to the Commissioners who administered the Act. The organization consisted of a large representative advisory council, which proved to be dead letter from the start, and the Committee, consisting of six scientific and three lay members with a full-time medical executive secretary.

There was some discussion about the policy to be followed: should the Committee concentrate on short-term specific problems, such as tuberculosis, or should it adopt a wider and deeper policy for support of medical research as opportunity arose? The benefits of the long-term policy that was adopted became immediately obvious on the outbreak of the war. The Committee was confronted by a diversity of unforeseen interests rather than problems of immediate concern to the medical practitioner. Thus, in addition to the straightforward concerns of illness in temperate climates, it had to work on tropical diseases, food rationing, wounds and wound infection, the physiology of working in submarines, the health of munitions workers, and so on.

To some extent, the success of the approach adopted by the Medical Research Committee influenced the structure and the operations of the DSIR. But the mission of the MRC was relatively straightforward, whereas the DSIR had come into being in the hurry of a national emergency, to meet a practical need rather than as a consequence of coherent policy. Both organizations figured large in the landmark report by Lord Haldane on the machinery of government.[22] This investigation, published in 1918, was an explicit response to the greatly increased involvement of central government – under pressure of wartime needs – in areas of national life where it had never before strayed.

Haldane's Committee dealt thoroughly with the problem of scientific research and its relations to government. The report distinguished between two types of research: the first was 'Research Work supervised by Administrative Departments'; the second was 'Research Work for General Use'. The first category covered the sort of research that would directly affect the business of individual departments and was clearly their direct responsibility, in the Committee's opinion.

The Committee cited as examples of the second category of research, the activities of the MRC and the DSIR. This kind of research was specifically designed for the advancement of knowledge. Haldane pointed out that 'science ignores departmental as well as geographical areas', that any organization concerned with general research must keep in touch with scientific workers of many fields and not only those where knowledge might be required for immediate *ad hoc* purposes, and that a general research organization must not be weighed down with the responsibility for implementing any recommendations that arose out of its research findings.

On the basis of these considerations, the Haldane Committee laid down two principles. First, that research for the advancement of knowledge should be established independently of the administrative departments concerned with its findings, and, secondly, that operational research – in the sense of work affecting the performance of a particular administrative department – should be the ordinary practice and responsibility of such departments. Haldane recommended that responsibility for the DSIR, and for the Medical Research Council, should remain in the hands of the Lord President of the Council, essentially the minister without portfolio, who would be the representative of science at Cabinet level. Haldane stressed that this structure for state support of scientific research: 'places responsibility to Parliament in the hands of a Minister who is . . . immune from any suspicion of being biased by administrative considerations against the application of the results of research'.

The Haldane recommendations of 1918 were the true foundation of the science research system in Britain, and determined its development over subsequent decades. By interposing independent research councils halfway between government departments on the one hand and research workers and their institutions on the other and by allowing these councils executive authority to administer funds at their sole discretion subject to parliamentary scrutiny, the system allowed the great creativity of basic science in Britain to continue throughout the period.

The most eloquent expression of the 'Haldane principle' comes not from Haldane himself but from Christopher Addison, Britain's first Minister of Health. In 1920, he piloted the bill through Parliament that set up the Ministry of Health. In accordance with the recommendations of the Haldane Committee, the old Medical Research Committee was not to be taken over as the research arm of the new ministry but set up independently of it as the Medical Research Council. This proposal was criticized and Addison replied in a memorandum that is worth quoting extensively:

A progressive Ministry of Health must necessarily become committed from time to time to particular systems of health administration . . . One does not wish to attach too much importance to the possibility that a particular Minister may hold strong personal views on particular questions of medical science or its application in practice; but even apart from special difficulties of this kind, which cannot be left out of account, a keen and energetic Minister will quite properly do his best to maintain the administrative policy which he finds existing in his department, or imposes on his department during his term of office. He would, therefore, be constantly tempted to endeavour in various ways to secure that the conclusions reached by organised research under any scientific body such as the Medical Research Committee, which was substantially under his control, should not suggest that his administrative policy might require alteration . . . It is essential that such a situation should not be allowed to arise, for it is the first object of scientific research of all kinds to make new discoveries, and these discoveries are bound to correct the conclusions based upon the knowledge that was previously available and, therefore, in the long run to make it right to alter administrative policy . . . This can only be secured by making the connexion between the administrative departments concerned, for example, with medicine and public health, and the research bodies whose work touches on the same subjects as elastic as possible, and by refraining from putting scientific bodies in any way under the direct control of Ministers responsible for the administration of health matters.[23]

This principle was to remain intact for half a century, until 1971, when Lord Rothschild initiated the Heath government's reorganizations of civil science by denying the very existence of such a principle.[24] One instance of the effect of ministerial control came in 1989 when a proposal to survey the sexual habits of the population, knowledge judged essential in the fight against the disease AIDS, was denied government funding apparently at the Prime Minister's direct order.[25] The work was later supported by a charity.

The end of the First World War saw the creation of one other institution that is crucial to the creativity of basic scientific research in Britain. Just as the state perceived a need for it to intervene in the business of science, so it also perceived a need for closer involvement in university education. This manifested itself in the establishment in 1919 of the University Grants Committee (now the Universities Funding Council).[26] Its role was to advise on how the single block sum voted annually by Parliament should be divided up among the universities.

In the institutions established at the end of the First World War, one can discern the beginnings of what came to be known as the 'dual support system'. The Department of Scientific and Industrial Research took over the pre-existing National Physical Laboratory and the Laboratory of the Government Chemist. It also set up a number of labs to carry out applied research relating to industry. But it did not establish its own laboratories for basic scientific research. Very slowly, there grew up a practice whereby the DSIR financed university scientists who had applied to it for funds to enable them to carry out a specific research project. But the DSIR did not need to pay the researchers' salaries, for that came out of the block grant from the University Grants Committee. And indeed, moneys from the UGC were sufficient to allow researchers to carry out inexpensive preliminary investigations to assess the potential of their ideas before they needed to apply to the DSIR. This system really came to fruition only in the years after 1945. Before the war the DSIR was not a major player in financing university research: only 81 research student grants were awarded in 1938–9 for the whole of Britain – there had been 24 in 1917 – restricting access to a research degree to those with other sources of income.[27]

The Medical Research Council and, when it was established in 1931, the Agricultural Research Council, did tend to set up their own laboratories for pure research, but they too helped support university scientists. This plurality of sources of funds helped further insulate the basic scientist from the changing distractions of practical affairs and enhanced the creativity for which British science has an enviable reputation.

By 1920, therefore, the form of the institutions (research councils and UGC) and the basic principles that were to shape British science policy for the next seven decades were all in place. In the field of pure science, the independence of the researcher from the politician and his access to a plurality of sources of funds had been assured. The distinction between pure science, or 'research work for general use' in Haldane's terminology, and applied research to support the administrative work of government departments had been established. But the difficulties also showed themselves early. The decentralized model meant that coordination within government was difficult (indeed, in 1971, Lord Rothschild asserted that it was impossible),[28] and as, over the years, the civil administrative departments commanded increasing funds to finance research, the role of the DSIR was relatively diminished. The hoped-for diffusion of knowledge and of expertise for the purpose of economic development proved difficult also as the excessive secrecy of the military service departments obstructed the full civil application of research paid for by the taxpayer; and, although the research associations were necessary, they were not by themselves sufficient to improve British industry's ability to innovate.

The Medical and Agricultural Research Councils, and the University Grants Committee all had relatively straightforward, single-purpose missions and all survived and prospered where ultimately the DSIR failed and was abolished in 1964. Only in the late 1980s were the role and very existence of the research councils and the UGC to be reconsidered.

Why did the DSIR fail? The problem with the Haldane dispensation − and it is a question that remains unresolved today − is whether the institutions that have served basic scientific research so well are actually appropriate to the conduct of applied research and to seeing that the fruits of that applied research are carried through into new industrial processes and products.[29] The Department of Scientific and Industrial Research had no counterpart to the Ministry of Health or of Agriculture which allowed a clear division of responsibilities between administrative department and research council. Its research associations never worked satisfactorily. Moreover they, and indeed the department itself, reflected a refusal by government to assume responsibility for industrial policy as well as scientific policy. It was not just research in chemistry that was deficient at the beginning of the First World War, it was the British chemical industry. In that instance, the setting up of the British Dyestuffs Corporation represented a state venture into industrial policy-making. But it was not until the formation of ICI in 1926, that the British chemical industry came truly into the twentieth century.[30] If governments had chosen differently, the setting up of ICI might perhaps have been the model for other industries — small companies amalgamating to form larger industrial organizations with the financial and human resources to compete on the world scale and, as a subsidiary consequence, with the financial and human resources to conduct serious applied research and development programmes. It might have been possible to force the pace via a Department of Industrial Reorganization, say, which could have stood in the same relation to the DSIR as the Ministry of Health to the Medical Research Council. Instead, the DSIR tried to change industry through the vehicle of the industrial research associations and it failed. The fragmented nature of British industry, and the consequent difficulties that small companies had both in financing research and in exploiting its results, were recurrent themes in the DSIR's annual reports well into the mid-1950s.[31]

The extent of the failure of Britain to learn all the lessons of the First World War can be exemplified by two instances taken from the early years of the Second World War: penicillin and the atomic bomb. Penicillin is usually regarded as a great British success, yet it was American companies who gained the first patents to the manufacture of the drug. That its development and manufacture were delayed in Britain is again testimony to the inability of British industry to create fertile conditions that would allow it to capitalize on new scientific developments.[32]

In 1928, working at St Mary's Hospital London, Alexander Fleming observed penicillin's anti-bacterial activity. He published his discovery the following year. But it was not until nine years later, that Ernst Chain, a refugee from Hitler and working in Howard Florey's laboratory, tried to take further the work of Fleming's 1929 paper. The Medical Research Council turned down an application for a grant to support the work, so for two years it was the Rockefeller Foundation that provided the necessary funds. Chain and Howard Florey published their results in *The Lancet* in 1940 and, the following year, the results of a very successful clinical trial of the drug. The publications aroused comparatively little interest.

In contrast to penicillin, the development of atomic and nuclear physics had been an international affair, with all the scientific pieces falling into place and published in the open literature by late 1939 just before the outbreak of war.[33] But the turning point that set scientists on the road to the atomic bomb itself was a cogent three-page memorandum written in March 1940 by two refugee scientists who had fled to England, Otto Frisch and Rudolph Peierls. The Frisch—Peierls memorandum set out all the salient points for a bomb based on nearly pure uranium-235. This prompted the setting up of the so-called Maud Committee to investigate the technical feasibility of building the bomb.

The Maud Report on the atomic bomb and the second paper on penicillin both came in the summer of 1941. According to Margaret Gowing:

> From this point the stories show another parallel of great importance. Neither atomic weapons nor penicillin could be made in Britain. In both cases, it was necessary to turn to the US. In both cases, the technological gap between the two countries became painfully obvious and the immense scale and efficiency of American scientific and industrial resources made Britain, the scientific pioneer, a junior partner. In both cases this was to lead to great bitterness.[34]

In April 1941 Florey sought industrial help himself in the US, at the Department of Agriculture laboratory at Peoria, Illinois. With facilities undreamed of in Britain, this laboratory performed the R&D necessary to get penicillin into large-scale production. Peoria discovered another strain of penicillin which was more suitable for mass-production by deep fermentation than the Oxford—Fleming strain. Pfizer, which was not then a pharmaceutical company, worked out the chemical engineering and the American government organized large-scale production. The supply promised to Florey by the Americans for British use never came, so the Oxford team with ICI (which then was not a pharmaceutical company either) produced just enough penicillin for clinical trials. By 1944, output covered British wartime military needs, albeit from a series of small bottle and tray plants in all kinds of old buildings. The future clearly lay with the American deep fermentation plants and British firms took licences to acquire US know-how. Gowing concludes her assessment of the story with the remark that:

> This Anglo-American collaboration led to the charge that Florey had given away patent rights on a British discovery to the USA. There had in 1942 been an explicit decision that an Oxford patent application would have been unethical, but it is doubtful if the production process as it then existed could have been covered by patents anyway. The American patents covered the production process which was the fruit of their resources and of superb chemical engineering.[35]

The parallel story of the atomic bomb is so well known that it hardly needs to be reiterated here. But one point must be stressed at the outset: few in the heady days after the war seem to have realized that it was not a scientific triumph at all: the basic science had been written down in the Frisch—Peierls memorandum, before the American project started. The building of the bomb was, like the manufacture of penicillin, a masterpiece of applied research, engineering and project management.

The British effort on the bomb was pursued half-heartedly after the Maud Committee had finished whereas the Americans, stimulated by the Frisch—Peierls memorandum and by the Maud Committee report, had set up a massive military—industrial complex, the Manhattan Engineering District. The British, who had declined to cooperate in 1941, found themselves behind in 1943, and were only reluctantly admitted as junior partners to the Manhattan Project. The extent of the British contribution was not widely publicized within US government circles, leading at the end of the war to Britain's exclusion from atomic secrets by the US Atomic Energy Act, the McMahon Act, which made little distinction between the UK and the USSR as far as nuclear military matters were concerned. The end of the war left both countries cherishing their own illusions: the Americans that they had done it all by themselves; the British, that the Americans could not have done it without them. These illusions, and the mis-identification of the bomb project as scientific rather than industrial, were damagingly to distort the priorities of the British government's science policy after the war.

Notes

1 On 1 October 1963, Mr Wilson told the Labour Party Conference, 'We are redefining and we are restating our socialism in terms of the scientific revolution ... The Britain that is going to be forged in the white heat of this revolution will be no place for restrictive practices or outdated methods on either side of industry.' The rhetoric slid effortlessly from science to industry and economic development.

2 Civil Research and Development, First Report of the House of Lords Select Committee on Science and Technology, 1986–87 Session (HMSO, 1986).

3 The remark was reported to have been made by a senior Treasury official to Sir George Porter, President of the Royal Society.

4 For example, Martin Ince, *The Politics of British Science* (Wheatsheaf, 1986) and Tam Dalyell *A Science Policy for Britain* (Longman, 1983). Tam Dalyell has played a leading role in the Labour Party's deliberations on science policy since the early 1960s, so he is intimately acquainted with the historical development of policy, but he makes only passing references in his book.

5 Margaret Gowing, 'The history of science, politics, and political economy', in *Information Sources in the History of Science and Medicine*, ed. Pietro Corsi and Paul Weindling (Butterworths, 1983), p. 99.

6 Ian Varcoe, *Organising for Science in Britain* (OUP, 1974).

7 Martin Wiener, *English Culture and the Decline of the Industrial Spirit 1850–1980* (CUP, 1981) and Stephen Cotgrove, *Technical Education and Social Change* (Allen and Unwin, 1958).

8 See Correlli Barnett, *The Audit of War* (Macmillan, 1986) for one polemical view of Britain's industrial inadequacies.

9 D. S. L. Cardwell, *The Organisation of Science in England* (Heinemann, 1957).

10 John Ziman, *The Force of Knowledge* (CUP, 1976).

11 Cardinal Newman, 'The idea of a university.'

12 The 1986 and 1987 Nobel Prizes in physics, for example, went to research guided mainly by West German scientists.

13 This point was made by Dr Max Perutz in a submission to the

Royal Society in response to the Morris Report to the Advisory Board for the Research Councils. Parts of the letter are quoted in *The Daily Telegraph*, 23 September 1987.

14 C. P. Snow, *The Two Cultures* (CUP, 1964).

15 Hilary Rose and Stephen Rose, *Science and Society* (Allen Lane, The Penguin Press, 1969).

16 Cardwell, *Organisation of Science*, p. 22.

17 Varcoe, *Organising for Science*.

18 Ibid.

19 Advisory Council on Science and Technology, Defence R&D: a National Resource, Report of a Working Group chaired by Sir Charles Reece (HMSO, 1989).

20 The argument at this point follows Varcoe, *Organising for Science*.

21 This account of the origins of the Medical Research Council is based on Sir Harold Himsworth, *The Development and Organisation of Scientific Knowledge* (Heinemann, 1970).

22 Report of the Machinery of Government Committee (The Haldane Report), ch. 4, Cd 9230 (HMSO, 1918).

23 Memorandum on the Ministry of Health Bill, 1919, as to the Work of the Medical Research Committee, Cmd 69 (HMSO, 1919).

24 The Organisation and Management of Government Research and Development (The Rothschild Report), Cmnd 4814 (HMSO, 1971).

25 Nicholas Schoon, 'Doubt over £500,000 Sex Survey', *The Independent*, 13 September 1989.

26 After 70 years of independent existence, the UGC was transformed into the Universities Funding Council in 1989, with a more market-orientated remit.

27 Rose and Rose, *Science and Society*, p. 46.

28 Rothschild Report 1971.

29 Argument here follows Varcoe, *Organising for Science*.

30 W.J. Reader, *ICI: a History* (OUP, 1970).

31 DSIR, Report for the Year 1954–55, Cmd 9690 (HMSO, 1956), p. 21.

32 Margaret Gowing, 'Does the timing of scientific discovery matter?', in *Priorities in Research*, ed. Sir John Kendrew and Julian Shelley (Exerpta Medica Amsterdam, 1983).

33 See, for example, John Simpson, *The Independent Nuclear State* (Macmillan, 1983); Margaret Gowing, *Britain and Atomic Energy 1939–1945* (Macmillan, 1964); Richard G. Hewlett and Oscar E.

Anderson jnr, *The New World*, vol. 1 of the official history of the US Atomic Energy Commission (Pennsylvania State University Press, 1962), pp. 42–4.

34 Margaret Gowing, 'Does the timing of scientific discovery matter?'.
35 Ibid.

4 The Period of Promise: the Years 1945–1962

The experience of the Second World War had confirmed the lesson of the Great War: that organized science was a prerequisite of survival and eventual victory in armed conflict between nations. As the war drew to a close, scientists and civil servants alike were laying plans to channel the energies of the state's scientists to the economic battlefield. If science had helped Britain win the war, then it would also help Britain win against other nations as they competed to gain a share in the marketplaces of the world. But by the end of the war, the country was virtually bankrupt and its scientists exhausted.[1] Britain was no longer a great power, and its science, technology and industrial policy since 1945 has reflected a reluctant but inexorable retreat from the position of superpower on the world stage to that of a medium-sized European country.

None the less, at the end of the war, British industry appeared to be in a strong position. Britain had after all been on the winning side and had not suffered destruction from aerial bombardment comparable with Germany nor disruption due to enemy occupation as had France. Partly for these reasons and partly as a consequence of the perception that the application of science had helped Britain win the war, it was believed (falsely as we now know) that British industry was a leader even in advanced technology. There was a large aircraft industry, which had not suffered too badly from the bombing, and an advanced nuclear capability built up in partnership with the

USA. In the 1950s, the UK tried to continue this grander role, developing its own independent atomic bomb, civilian nuclear power and aircraft technology. The disproportionate share of government money devoted to R&D in nuclear power and in the aircraft industry became a firmly established distortion of the pattern of government spending that persisted through into the 1980s. Even as late as 1982, the Thatcher government, committed though it was to reducing public expenditure and to non-interference in industry, enshrined a large subsidy — called Launch Aid — to the aircraft industry as part of the Civil Aviation Act.[2] The seeds of this distortion were planted in the 1950s, a decade characterized by a mismatch between political and economic ambition, and economic and technological reality.[3] The result was a series of expensive and costly failures in advanced technology.

Little of that was apparent in 1945, when Clement Attlee's Labour government took over the reigns of power. Among the many other tasks it faced was that of rationalizing for the purposes of a peacetime economy the *ad hoc* structures that had grown up during the war to channel scientific advice and expertise to decision-makers.

The most important step in harnessing science for the purposes of the state — indeed the one that proved to be the country's salvation during the Second World War — had actually been taken nearly five years before hostilities broke out.[4] Dominating strategy in the 1930s was the idea that bomber aircraft had changed the nature of warfare and that there was no defence against them: no less a figure than Mr Baldwin himself had pronounced that 'the bomber will always get through.' Against this background, the Air Ministry set up a Committee for the Scientific Study of Air Defence, which met for the first time on 28 January 1935, under the chairmanship of Sir Henry Tizard, the Rector of Imperial College and former Secretary of the Department of Scientific and Industrial Research. It was this committee that took up the idea of radar (or radio direction finding as it was then known) and, in today's parlance, 'sold' the idea to the military.

In July 1938, Tizard suggested a Central Scientific Committee be set up to coordinate defence research currently being performed by the separate service ministries and by the DSIR.[5] In 1939, the Ministry of Supply set up an Advisory Committee on Scientific Research and Technical Development to concentrate on weapons research and engineering. A year after Tizard's memorandum, in July 1939, Sir William Bragg the then President of the Royal Society wrote to the Minister for Coordination of Defence offering to set up a committee of scientists to provide expert advice.[6] This led eventually to the establishment of a Scientific Advisory Committee to the War Cabinet, with Lord Hankey as Chairman.

But the committee was little more than a cipher. In reality, scientific advice to the wartime Cabinet was channelled through F. A. Lindemann, Lord Cherwell, who had a seat in the Cabinet as Paymaster General. More significant, however, than his office was the fact that he was on close personal terms with Churchill. The experience of having a Cabinet Minister who was, or had been, a practising scientist, and whose remit was to provide scientific advice to the Cabinet was a unique departure. The outcome was questionable: Lindemann was wrong on many important questions during the war. He opposed radar and he advocated blanket aerial bombing of German cities. Fortunately for the survival of the UK, he was defeated on the first issue; but he won on the second. His inaccurate calculations of the damage which could be inflicted provided part of the justification for the RAF's policy, even though better analyses existed. Had those more realistic calculations, by Tizard, P.M.S. Blackett and others, received due attention then hundreds of bomber crews might not have been sent to their deaths; nor would thousands of German civilians have perished; and some of Europe's finest cultural and architectural heritage would not have been reduced to rubble. Investigations after the war showed that the effort expended in bombing Germany had damaged the UK's war effort more than the bombs had affected the Germans' ability to continue to fight.[7]

Science was vital to the war effort, but owing to Lindemann's complex personality, its application was not uniform nor planned in the strategic manner that might have been possible. And even before Lindemann, as early as August 1940, Allen Lane the founder of Penguin books, published a famous and influential broadside against the confusion and neglect of science: a Penguin Special entitled, *Science in War*. The message printed in bold on the front cover was unequivocal: 'The full use of our scientific resources is essential if we are to win the war. Today they are being half used.'[8] The book, the authors of which were not named, was the product of the strangely named 'Tots and Quots' a London-based dining club organized by the biologist Solly Zuckerman.[9] Its membership had a distinctly left-wing flavour. It included J. D. Bernal, the Marxist crystallographer; Julian Huxley; Patrick Blackett; the biologists C. H. Waddington and C. D. Darlington; and the economist Roy Harrod. Also a member was the doyen of all British science journalism, J. G. Crowther.

The years before the outbreak of the Second World War had been times of ferment among scientists as they struggled to work out for themselves what the social role of science should be and then tried (unsuccessfully) to convince those in power to act on their conclusions. 'Tots and Quots' was but one of the progeny of those years. The landmark publication was J.D. Bernal's Marxist-orientated *The Social Function of Science* in 1939, which in part contrasted the benefits that would accrue from science centrally directed by the state, with the diversity and confusion that seemed to characterize British science policy in the 1930s.[10] Bernal, a crystallographer and communist, was one of the leading members of that 'Visible College' of scientists who were committed socialists and who dominated thinking about the relationship of science and the state in the 1930s.[11] One vehicle for their activities was the leftist-dominated Association of Scientific Workers, the trade union for practising scientists. Although it gained a new lease of life in the years before and just after the war, in the later post-war years the Association's role as spokesman for the interests of the professional scientist gradually eroded until in 1968 it merged with the technicians union to form ASTMS. Bernal was one of the founders of what might be termed 'the British school of crystallography' which lay behind much of the work that was to win Nobel Prizes in the post-war years, although his own research was never quite in the Nobel class.

Another member of the 1930s group and one who was to influence post-war science was Patrick Blackett. Blackett was one of the most distinguished protégés of Lord Rutherford at the Cavendish Laboratory in Cambridge; despite his left-wing views, he was invited to become a member of Tizard's committee that fostered the development of radar, and he worked on the science of operational research as applied to practical problems during the war. His physics research brought him the 1948 Nobel Prize, he acquired a peerage in the 1960s and eventually was elected President of the Royal Society.

In the late 1930s science was being promoted by left-wingers because of its perceived desirable practical effect on society. The actions of the Attlee government were to prove a disappointment, but much of the rhetoric of the Labour Party in the 1964 election campaign was pure Bernalism. It is a measure of how much these ideas have become commonplace that in the 1980s, the Conservative government set about re-shaping British science precisely because it was not perceived to have delivered that practical effect. A further irony is that, in the view of some scientists who spent their formative years under the 'hands-off' Haldane dispensation of the 1930s to 1960s, the new arrangements that are developing for British science towards the end of the century represent a highly centralized direction and control, so much so that one very eminent scientist has dismissed the changes as 'the new Marxism'.[12]

The vital importance of science to the country's economic well-being was a commonplace across the political spectrum in the aftermath of the Second World War. In December 1945, the Attlee government appointed a committee under Sir Alan Barlow, then Second Secretary to the Treasury, to look into the feared shortage of scientific manpower. The Committee took the case for science as self-evident:

> We do not think that it is necessary to preface our report by stating at length the case for developing our scientific resources. Never before has the importance of science been more widely

recognised or so many hopes of future progress and welfare founded upon the scientist. Least of all nations can Great Britain afford to neglect whatever benefits the scientists can confer upon her. If we are to maintain our position in the world and restore and improve our standard of living, we have no alternative but to strive for that scientific achievement without which our trade will wither, our colonial Empire will remain undeveloped and our lives and freedom will be at the mercy of a potential aggressor.[13]

But despite the discussions before the war, and in contrast to the situation that prevailed at the time of the First World War, the scientists themselves were unable to agree on the details of what should be done in the aftermath of the Second World War. According to Ian Varcoe: 'The post-war transformation of the relations between Government and Science involved no major reorganisation of the Government's organisation for promoting and supporting scientific research.'[14] The major issues that were to dominate subsequent thinking about a policy for science were only dimly perceived before 1964. The scientists were deeply divided on the issues and were unable to present a collective view about the problems or to provide a concerted response to subsequent central initiatives in the field of civil research. Yet, as noted in chapter 3, tensions already existed within the government system: between the military and the civil departments; between the commissioning of civil research to further a department's administrative purposes and the performance of general research work; and between the commissioning of research for the government's own use and the commissioning of research using government money but intended to benefit industry. These tensions would grow as administrative departments spent increasing amounts of money on research without there being an overall analysis and consequent policy to control spending.

The Association of Scientific Workers, for all its centralizing zeal, rejected the suggestion of a Ministry of Science.[15] It argued for a Central Scientific Office at Cabinet level, maintaining that if all scientific work were done in a single ministry, 'the rest of the Ministries would be divorced from science and the valuable responsibility of Ministers for an essential element of their own work would be lost.' In the end, the Lord President of the Council continued his pre-war role as a non-departmental minister for science.

In one sense at least, the post-war structures needed to deal with science — both with the education of scientists and with research — were only put in place in 1964. The three major pillars of the civil research system — the Department of Scientific and Industrial Research, the Medical Research Council and the Agricultural Research Council — all continued to perform much the same functions as they had in the years before the war. The dual-support system continued and flourished with the expansion of the universities in the post-war period. The 1950s are in some respects barren years, therefore. What changes did occur tended to be *ad hoc* adjustments to accommodate the growth in science rather than a serious overhaul of the system. That only came with the realization that important areas of research were undeveloped because there were no agencies to support them and when the proliferation of other bodies financing research exposed the painful inadequacies of the Department of Scientific and Industrial Research.

Nonetheless, there were changes in the immediate post-war years. Bernal himself observed in 1945 that:

> the habit of attaching scientific advisors and scientific advisory committees is now spreading. The outline of a new system of research organisation is becoming visible. The addition of a scientific section means that the activity of the Ministry need no longer depend on the routine of an office, on the vagaries of a Minister's career, or on the vigour of critics in the House of Commons.[16]

The scientific services of the various ministries increased considerably, with the number of specialist advisory committees rising from 200 in 1939 to 700 by 1949.

The post-war expansion of science was massive.[17] In the 17 years from 1945–6 to 1962–3, government expenditure on civil science rose from £6.58 million to £151.6 million. These figures are in money terms, not real terms, but even when allowance is made for inflation, the 1962–3 figures represent at least ten times as much activity as in 1945. At least half of the expenditure in 1962 was on areas of science and technology, such as civil atomic energy and space research, which had not existed before the war.

British industry itself was doing more research both from its own resources and through government-sponsored schemes. By 1963, the year before its abolition, the Department of Scientific and Industrial Research was supporting 53 different industrial research associations, more than two and a half times the number in existence at the end of the war. This contrasts with the unhappy record of the inter-war years, when the DSIR ended up with just 21 research associations in 1940, fewer than it had had in 1923.

The success story of the Attlee government was in the education and training of scientists. Sir Alan Barlow's Committee recommended that the output of professional scientists, then estimated to be about 2,500 a year, should be doubled.[18] The Committee thought that the task would take five to ten years. In the event, the target was reached in only four. The Barlow Committee also commended the idea of creating two or three institutes of technology, of the quality and standing of the Massachusetts and California Institutes of Technology in the USA. This proposal has never been given true effect. Once again, an opportunity to come to terms with the new institutions that were and are needed to support science in the twentieth century was lost. However, the Barlow Committee's main recommendation, that the government should make more money available to allow the universities to expand, was accepted and acted upon by the government. Oxford and Cambridge universities were obstructive. They informed the Barlow Committee that they could not expand to cater for any more than their pre-war student numbers without there being a drop in academic standards. Over the post-war period, however, these two institutions have not been slow to accept government or private money and to expand their student numbers accordingly.

Lord Zuckerman's memoirs reveal just how spurious these objections were.[19] Some time after the war, when the supply of scientific manpower was again being debated, Sir James Chadwick, the Cambridge physicist, and Sir Cyril Hinshelwood the Oxford chemist (both of them Nobel Prize-winners) 'were inclined to argue that the entry examination papers for Oxford or Cambridge should be regarded as a national yardstick'. Zuckerman recalls that after one such meeting the distinguished physicist Sir John Cockroft (also a Nobel Prize-winner) sent him a set of entrance papers to a Cambridge college with the covering note: 'Could you get in? I couldn't.'

The Attlee government faced a bewildering variety of scientific advisory committees when it took office. They included the Scientific Advisory Committee to the War Cabinet; the Ministry of Supply's Advisory Committee on Scientific Research and Technical Development; and the Central Register of Scientific Manpower under the Ministry of Labour. Actual scientific research was being administered and carried out by the DSIR and the other research councils in their laboratories, and in the research establishments belonging to the service ministries.

The government made only three significant changes to the administration of science after the war. The first, in 1947, was to set up an Advisory Council on Scientific Policy to cover civil science, and a Defence Research Policy Committee to deal with military science.[20]

The first chairman of the Advisory Council on Scientific Policy was Sir Henry Tizard, who also chaired the Defence Research Policy Committee. For six years, therefore, there was a connection between the civil and military policy towards state-supported science and the possibility that the two aspects might be coordinated. According to Lord Zuckerman's memoirs, there was an understanding that, on Sir Henry's retirement, Sir John Cockroft would succeed as chairman of both committees.[21] This arrangement was interrupted by the return of the Churchill government in 1951 and the antipathy of Churchill's personal scientific adviser, Lord Cherwell, to the civil Advisory Council on Scientific Policy (ACSP). Sir John Cockroft duly became head of the Defence Research Policy

Committee, but chairmanship of the ACSP went to Alexander Todd, professor of chemistry at Cambridge. A distinguished scientist, he was awarded the Nobel Prize in 1957, and later became Lord Todd and President of the Royal Society. He continued as chairman of the ACSP until it was dissolved in 1964.

The ACSP consisted of the secretaries of the research councils (which for this purpose includes the DSIR), the chairman of the University Grants Committee, a Treasury representative (initially, Sir Alan Barlow) and an equal number of independent scientists and scientific industrialists. This body has continued in one guise or another more or less continuously ever since. In the early years, it was particularly concerned with the supply (or rather perceived shortage of supply) of scientific manpower, and it maintained a permanent subcommittee on this topic. The ACSP published annual reports. (Its present-day successor, the Advisory Council on Science and Technology (ACOST) is a much more secretive beast, which has declined to publish broad general statements on science policy and apparently believes that it has more influence if it gives confidential advice to government. Whether the results bear this out is not a question that can be answered in this book. Under pressure from a House of Lords Select Committee report in 1990, ACOST is now committed to publishing a general report every three years or so.)

Zuckerman became deputy chairman of the ACSP, a post which he retained until its abolition. He also chaired the sub-committee that dealt with estimates of scientific manpower, its supply and demand. But in his judgement:

Little that we discussed was, however, significant politically. Attlee, by whom the Council was set up, does not refer to it in his autobiography. As Prime Minister, the matters that came before the Council were of little or no political interest to him. Throughout its existence it found itself impotent and often balked when it came to advising either about the use of scientific and technological resources in executive Departments of State or about the programmes of the research councils.[22]

It is not clear that any of the Council's successor bodies have been more successful.

The Attlee government's second innovation was the brainchild of Patrick Blackett.[23] In 1948, under the Development of Inventions Act, the government set up the National Research Development Corporation (NRDC) to foster the development of inventions that would not otherwise attract financial backing from private sources. The NRDC was also given the right of first refusal to patent the fruits of research supported by public funds, thereby establishing a mechanism for the taxpayer to benefit from the development of work financially supported by the state. The establishment of the NRDC was a conscious attempt to break what was then already perceived to be a prevailing British disease: the British are good at inventing things, but poor at turning them into products that customers would like to buy. The NRDC was financed by advances from the Board of Trade. But, in principle, the NRDC was an independent body, free to operate on normal commercial lines, providing that in the long term it covered its costs.

The NRDC had a great success in the early 1950s with the cephalosporin group of antibiotics. Royalties worth more than £150 million have been received from cephalosporin, and shared between the NRDC and the inventors. But, in 1958, it made a serious error of judgement in the amount of money it spent backing Sir Christopher Cockerill's hovercraft. The promise of these amphibious vehicles has never been realized: they were too costly, consumed too much fuel and required extensive maintenance. The NRDC spent £8 million in promoting their development and, 30 years later, had not recouped the money until, in 1990, the NRDC's successor succeeded in litigation over an alleged infringement of hovercraft patents by the US Department of Defense which uses air-cushioned landing craft.[24] The royalty payments that should flow from this decision will finally allow the investment to be recouped.

By 1963, the NRDC's annual deficit was running at £250,000. However, at this time, the corporation made its best investment – just at the point when its commitment to the hovercraft was heaviest. In 1962, it started to contribute funding to work on pyrethrin insecticides being carried out at the Agricultural Research Council's Rothampstead Experimental Station. Synthetic pyrethrins now account for a quarter of the global market for insecticides, and the patents on these compounds were the single most productive group of British patents registered since the war. Although NRDC's funding started in 1962, it was only in 1973 that a team led by Dr Michael Elliott developed the main products. They are synthetic analogues derived from the pyrethrum naturally present in flowers of the chrysanthemum. The first commercial products appeared in the late 1970s.

However, in the early 1980s, the NRDC became embroiled in another controversy, this time over its failure to patent the rights to monoclonal antibodies discovered by Cesar Milstein and Georges Kohler, who later gained the Nobel Prize in recognition of their work, at the MRC's Laboratory for Molecular Biology in Cambridge. The technique of monoclonal antibodies is vital to many of the methods used by biotechnology companies around the world to develop new products. There is some dispute as to whether the failure to secure a patent was entirely the NRDC's fault, but in 1985 it was amalgamated with the National Enterprise Board to form British Technology Group (BTG), and it lost the right of first refusal to patent discoveries arising from publicly funded science. By the late 1980s, the highly profitable patents from cephalosporin and the insecticides were expiring. The Conservative government is keen to privatize the organization possibly by encouraging a management buy-out.

The third agency established in the immediate aftermath of the Second World War was the Nature Conservancy. The brain-child of Sir Julian Huxley, who had campaigned for such an organization for a quarter of a century, it had a dual role: to establish nature reserves and national parks; and to finance research on nature conservation, work that today would be termed environmental research. But the quantity of research funded by the Nature Conservancy was tiny. Even in 1962–3, it amounted only to about £600,000. Eventually the responsibility for research and for conservation were to be separated, but in the 1980s the future of the conservation body became a subject of controversy. In 1989, one of Mr Nicholas Ridley's last acts as Secretary of State for the Environment was to propose the break-up of the Nature Conservancy Council into three regional bodies.

The Attlee government encouraged two further smaller developments. One was to promote the formation of chief scientists divisions within relevant administrative departments. But with the exception of the Ministry of Defence, which is outside the remit of this book, the chief scientists exercised little power until the Rothschild reforms of the early 1970s. The second change, in 1945, was to adopt a taxation policy giving industry incentives to join or to form industrial research associations. At least on the surface, this policy was successful. By 1955, some 20,000 companies representing half of British industry were members of 39 research associations. In 1956, the government contributed £1.3 million to the £4.7 million total income that the research associations enjoyed. That year they employed 1,500 graduates, nearly three times as many as they had at the end of the war.

As early as 1947, however, some voices were heard to say that the government's administration of science was in a mess. The Commons Select Committee on the Estimates that year remarked that there was no clear demarcation of function between the DSIR and the administrative departments in commissioning research.[25] The Committee concluded that it was 'too early to decide what the ideal Government organisation for research should be'. But it was clear that even in the years immediately after the war, the relative independence of the research councils – guaranteed them by the operation of the Haldane principle – was being questioned.[26] Some advocated handing over a significant fraction of the councils' responsibilities to the executive departments of state – an idea whose time was to come in 1971 with Lord Rothschild's reorganization of civil research and development. But the research councils retained their independence when, in 1948, the Advisory Council on Scientific Policy attempted to define the role of the DSIR. The administrative departments should be free to identify problems, settle their own priorities and decide from whom to commission research and how to apply the results. The DSIR was to be relegated to conducting background research and to work done on commission from the administrative departments.[27] Over the years that followed, the DSIR failed to assert and find a role for itself. It was eclipsed not only by the administrative departments but also by the *ad hoc* growth of other bodies that disposed of large sums of money for research.

After the reforms of the Attlee years, the return of a Conservative government in 1951 marked the beginning of a period in which it appeared no longer so urgent that the government and science should have such an intimate relationship. The influence of Lord Cherwell came to the fore once again, precipitating the resignation of Sir Henry Tizard from the two science policy committees and, as noted earlier, the damaging separation of defence from civil science.

In 1952, the Conservative government announced that one technological institution was to assume university rank: a partial fulfilment of the Barlow Committee's recommendation nearly seven years earlier that the UK should set up institutions comparable in standing and remit to the California Institute of Technology and the Massachusetts Institute of Technology. But the decision was little more than window dressing, for the institution chosen was Imperial College which was already a part of the University of London. A dreary succession of half-hearted measures followed in successive years, each of them shrinking from the challenge of transforming Britain's universities into institutions capable of providing scientifically and technologically educated manpower in the large numbers that the country needed; each of them instead purveying the fiction that the country's need for technically competent manpower could be satisfied on the cheap, in particular by educating engineers to a lower level than university degree with the award of Higher National Diplomas and the like. The seeds of the ludicrous 'binary divide' which currently flourishes between polytechnics and universities were planted in these years.

Throughout the 1950s, government spending on civil science continued to grow, but no efforts were made to develop and expand the apparatus to control and direct policy and to ensure that money was being wisely spent. Instead, eye-catching prestige projects — which inevitably meant disproportionately expensive projects — began to account for much of the science budget. In pure science, for example, the large Jodrell Bank radio telescope ran up a deficit of more than a quarter of a million pounds;[28] while on the applied side, aircraft and atomic energy (both military and civil) diverted money and manpower away from other projects.

The two most significant institutions in these years were the Ministry of Aviation and the Atomic Energy Authority. By 1962–3, the UKAEA was spending £50 million a year on civil research and development (it was also responsible for spending an unknown amount of money on Britain's military nuclear programme at that time). As well as its responsibilities for aircraft development, the Ministry of Aviation was also the lead organization in financing electronics research and development during the 1950s. Its civil research and development budget stood at nearly £25 million in 1962–3. This compares with the DSIR's expenditure then of just over £21 million.[29]

The Atomic Energy Authority was set up in 1954. At the end of the war, responsibility for work on atomic energy was transferred from the Department of Scientific and Industrial Research to the Ministry of Supply (whose present-day descendant roughly speaking is the procurement executive of the Ministry of Defence). This was formalized by the 1946 Atomic Energy Act and continued until the functions were transferred back to the Lord President of the Council in January 1954 as part of the preparations for the establishment of the Authority in June 1954.

The government's reasoning was set out in a White Paper published in November 1953.[30] It believed that a non-departmental organization was needed because 'as the industrial uses of atomic energy become relatively more prominent, the case for a form of control of the project which is more akin to the structure of a big industrial organisation than to that of a Government department becomes increasingly strong.' The government also noted 'that all the other countries working in this field have adopted some special form of organisation, outside the

normal framework of an ordinary Government department.'
On its formation, the Authority's budget was some £50 million.
This covered both civil and military research and also the
production of nuclear materials for Britain's nuclear weapons
programme. It employed some 24,000 staff, among the most
skilled engineers, scientists and craftsmen in the country.

The rights and wrongs of the decision by the Attlee government that Britain should build its own nuclear weapons have
been endlessly debated and are not relevant here. Few voices
were raised against the policy at the time. One of them was Sir
Henry Tizard.[31] Tizard was sceptical of the bomb's usefulness
to the UK and feared (rightly as it turned out) that the effort
involved in making it and the diversion of scientific resources
that it would involve would accelerate the country's decline
into second-power status. The scale of the effort involved
questions not just of money, but also of skilled manpower.
Throughout the 1950s, policy-makers were obsessed by what
they perceived as a shortage of trained scientific manpower.
Yet the decision to develop nuclear weapons, and later to build
civil nuclear power stations, diverted thousands of skilled
scientists and engineers away from private industry where their
expertise might have been turned to the development of products that would have contributed to the country's exports and
economic advantage. Instead, the most attractive and technically
challenging enterprise of the 1950s was a state supported venture
with two products. One, nuclear weapons, was vastly expensive
to obtain but once they were built they were economically
unproductive. The other product, civil nuclear power stations
for generating electricity, whose development had been encouraged and financed by the state, had only one customer: the
state. As a result, many of the brightest of an entire generation
of scientists and engineers were employed on activities that
were either economically redundant or were free of the discipline
of having to make products that were better than a rival
company's.

In the event, the line of civil reactors developed in the UK
seems to have brought little economic benefit to the country. A
couple of the first-generation reactors, known as Magnox, were

sold abroad to Italy and to Japan, but there were no further orders and the second-generation design, the advanced gas-cooled reactor, proved a complete failure commercially. In the mid-1970s, the then chairman of the Central Electricity Generating Board, Arthur Hawkins, remarked that the development of the advanced gas-cooled reactor was 'a disaster we must never repeat'. By the mid-1970s, the CEGB wanted to abandon the British technology and buy in American. The first of these reactors, licensed from the Westinghouse corporation of the USA, is now being constructed at Sizewell in Suffolk. However, maintenance of a nuclear programme came into conflict with Mrs Thatcher's aim of privatizing the electricity supply industry, and privatization won out over arguments that nuclear sources might be needed to ensure a diversity of supply of electricity or that nuclear power was a form of generation that did not directly contribute to the 'greenhouse effect'. Late in 1989 the government announced that it would not proceed with any further reactor building after Sizewell.[32] The situation is to be reviewed in 1994. The cost to the nation in monetary terms of this wasted research effort is almost impossible to estimate. But the cost in terms of opportunities lost because researchers were not being employed on more productive tasks is literally incalculable.

The case of the aircraft industry is more complex.[33] It did produce aircraft, such as the Comet, that were technologically excellent and had the potential to be economically competitive. But, in the end, the Comet lost out to the Boeing 707. The one success of the 1950s was the turbo-prop Viscount. The Comet, Britannia, Vanguard and VC10 were all commercial failures. In the military arena, the TSR2 also was a failure. The sorry story was repeated with Britain's abortive rocket programme and the abandoned Blue Streak and Black Knight rockets. The aeroindustry's final white elephant was the artefact not of the UK alone but of France also: Concorde.

If aviation and atomic energy were the two big spenders throughout the 1950s, other government bodies were also commissioning research on a significant scale. The General Post Office's Dollis Hill research station was employing 241 research officers by 1961, about a third of the total on the payroll of the DSIR. By 1963, the GPO was financing research to the tune of £5 million annually.

British industry had continued its dismal record of failing to invest in high technology. Many companies were content to take out licences to market new products that American companies had developed in their corporate laboratories. As early as the 1930s, US companies had been opening research laboratories in Britain and, as noted in chapter 3, the development of penicillin was funded by an American charity when British funding bodies proved reluctant. In the immediate post-war years, Britain's industrial research associations benefited from US government aid: more than $800,000 was made available under the US technical assistance programmes after the war, mainly to provide scientific equipment and machine tools not otherwise available in Europe.[34]

But a more ominous development for the competitiveness of British industry was the increasing interest that commercial firms were taking in the UK. The American desire to breach tariff barriers had led to a total American investment in UK industry of $941 million by 1955. And the Americans were quick to appreciate that British science was worth investing in. According to Armytage:

> the American research laboratory became a familiar feature in England, especially after the Second World War. By 1958, it is estimated that almost a quarter of the $5,600 million which American industry spent on private research and development was made directly available to the United Kingdom; more than the whole of the British Industry and the Co-operative Research Associations spent annually on research.[35]

That trend continues to the present day. In 1987, for example, the American computer company IBM spent more on its research, development and engineering than the whole of British industry.[36]

Even basic scientific research was beginning to increase in scale and cost. In particular, the investigation of the fundamental constituents of matter — nuclear and subnuclear physics — was requiring ever larger and more expensive equipment. It is one of the quirks of physics that the investigation of the smallest entities known to science require the largest machines and most elaborate pieces of scientific apparatus in existence.

Before the war, the Cavendish Laboratory had been the centre of British research into nuclear and subnuclear physics. But shortly after Neville Mott took over as director in 1954, he vetoed the proposed building of a linear accelerator that would have kept the laboratory in that line of business.[37] Instead, he changed the direction of the laboratory to focus more on topics of solid-state physics and the like, which did not then require the large machines necessary for subnuclear physics. With the benefit of hindsight one can see that the research laboratory structure was no longer adequate to cope with the demands of 'big science' of which subnuclear physics was the first example. But the decisions which followed from within the British scientific community do not seem to have lead to a creative and productive new system for fostering worthwhile research in the era of 'big science'.

The 1950s seem to mark the beginning of the end of the Cavendish's pre-eminence in international science. Several of its scientists were to become Nobel laureates, but almost all of them for work that had already begun before 1950. Few scientists who began their career in the Cavendish in the 1950s have made the trip to Stockholm.

The increasing cost of research into the constituents of the atomic nucleus led to the formation, in March 1957, of the National Institute for Research in Nuclear Science (NIRNS). This was established to provide facilities for common use by all universities carrying on research into subnuclear physics.[38] The research differed considerably from that carried out by the Atomic Energy Authority. The AEA was interested in the properties of a very few atomic nuclei — mainly uranium and plutonium — and with the practical application of that knowledge to weapons or to the construction of nuclear power stations. NIRNS was set up to investigate the properties of other nuclei and more especially to probe what smaller layers of structure might be contained within the nucleus: the so-called subatomic or elementary particles. The researchers sometimes conveniently blurred this distinction for the benefits of parliamentary pay-masters, since more money was likely to flow if politicians believed that another source of energy even more powerful than that of the bomb might be discovered via this research. Of course, since it was curiosity-driven work, no such application has been forthcoming.

NIRNS was financed initially through the Atomic Energy Vote and in May 1958 was granted its own Royal Charter. By 1962–3 it was spending about £7 million a year. Although NIRNS was intended to provide a common-user facility, it might nonetheless have seemed logical to site it in close prox-imity to the Cavendish at Cambridge, where the majority of the particle physicists in the country had some association. Instead, its prestige project, a particle accelerator called Nimrod, was built not far from Oxford, a university with little tradition in the subject. The new facility, which is now called the Ruther-ford Appleton laboratory, is adjacent to the UK Atomic Energy Authority's Harwell establishment which conducts research into an entirely different discipline. One of the quainter side effects of its situation was that for some time anyone wishing to telephone the country's most advanced laboratory for subnuclear physics had to place trunk calls via one of the last manual telephone exchanges in England.

In the event, Nimrod itself was rendered largely redundant by developments at CERN, the European Laboratory for particle physics near Geneva, Switzerland.[39] The principal machine in both laboratories was an accelerator of the type known as a proton synchrotron, but the CERN machine first operated in 1959 whereas Nimrod first accelerated protons to its maximum design energy only in 1963. Moreover, the CERN machine was capable of accelerating its subatomic projectiles to energies that were nearly four times higher than those achieved by Nimrod: 28 thousand million electron volts (GeV) compared to Nimrod's 7 GeV. This inevitably meant that all the pioneering physics was done at CERN (or in similar US facilities) and little in the way of good physics came out of the Rutherford

Laboratory at this time. Ironically, the leader of the team which built the CERN machine and who was in no small measure responsible for its excellence was a British engineer, Sir John Adams. In the 1980s, Nimrod was cannibalized to convert it into a source of one particular type of subnuclear particle, called a neutron. These are used, not to probe the fundamental structure of matter, but to investigate the properties of bulk solids. In its new guise as the Spallation Neutron Source (also known as ISIS), the facility is for the first time in the forefront of world research.

In 1962, NIRNS was given permission to build another large common-user facility, this time an electron accelerator. This machine, called Nina, was sited at the Daresbury Laboratory established in a greenfield site not far from Runcorn in Cheshire. Nina too provided little that was memorable, and it operated for only ten years, from 1967 to 1977. It also was cannibalized and converted into a synchrotron radiation facility, essentially a giant X-ray machine for investigating crystal structures, especially of biological origin. It started operations as the Synchrotron Radiation Source in 1980. By the 1980s, therefore, both biology and solid-state physics had themselves been transformed from the sort of 'little science' that could be done in one university-supported laboratory into 'big science' that required large and expensive common-user facilities, just as particle physics had required some 20 years previously. Although the redundant particle accelerators were refashioned for use in solid-state physics and biology, the poverty of the policy of establishing laboratories far from the university-based researchers who were going to use them was finally acknowledged in the 1980s, and a new mechanism for the support of science was introduced: the Interdisciplinary Research Centre based at a single university campus.[40]

The final development of note in the 1950s was the announcement by the government in 1958 of a programme of space research. As this included rockets and satellites, the programme was placed with the Ministry of Aviation rather than the Department of Scientific and Industrial Research. This despite the fact that space research depends on many disciplines, including telemetry and data processing, that the DSIR was involved in. By 1962–3 the government was spending £1.2 million on space research (not including the country's subscription to the international rocket-making agency: ELDO, the European Launcher Development Organization).

In 1959, an Overseas Research Council was formed to advise on research policy with regard to countries both within and outside the Commonwealth countries. However, it had no money at its disposal to finance research, its role was purely advisory. One other unusual organization that was funding research throughout this period was the Development Commission, which had been set up under the road improvement Acts of 1909 and 1910. By 1962–3 it was spending about £800,000 a year on research in fisheries, oceanography, sociology and rural development. As such, its research spending was greater than that of the Nature Conservancy.

Throughout the 1950s, only two attempts were made to try to bring order to the unruly growth of institutions and agencies. The first in 1955 was half-hearted: a committee of enquiry under Sir Harry Jephcott, then chairman and managing director of Glaxo, reported on the internal structure of the DSIR.[41] It noted that the department was 'inadequate to secure the most effective use of [its] resources in the national interest. Much is started; not enough is stopped. As a result many of the programmes have become too diffuse or uneven in quality.' However, all that the Committee could come up with was a proposal to strengthen the Advisory Council which oversaw the DSIR's work, turning it into an executive council.

The second attempt was political and led, in 1959, to the appointment of Lord Hailsham as Britain's first (and last) Minister for Science. As Lord Hailsham was also Lord President of the Council and therefore already responsible for the DSIR, and the research councils, the creation of the new post was not perhaps as significant as it might have seemed. None the less it did represent an attempt to bring under the political control of one minister the disparate parts of the empire of science that had grown up since the war. It also provided a focus for coordinating British participation in the various international scientific projects, such as CERN, the International Atomic Energy Agency, and the European Space Research Organization, that the country had joined during the 1950s. But the appointment fell a long way short of what was needed to coordinate science funding and establish priorities and, more damagingly, of getting the fruits of science into British industry. In one devastating phrase, *The Economist* newspaper dismissed the office of the Minister for Science as a 'palsied little creation'.[42] The Federation of British Industry advocated a more powerful central administrative organization than the office of the Minister for Science, echoing the sentiments of *The Observer* newspaper in 1959, 'The first essential in this country is for science to penetrate more widely and thoroughly into the more backward industries.'[43] The most serious omission perhaps from Lord Hailsham's portfolio was that he had no responsibility for the scientific functions of the Aviation Ministry, one of the highest spenders at the time. In a Commons debate, Aubrey Jones MP advocated amalgamating all these functions within a Ministry of Science and Technology, based on the research side of the Ministry of Aviation.[44] But that was not to be until the Labour government of Harold Wilson set up its Ministry of Technology.

It was apparent that the job was not like that of other Ministers. As Hailsham himself put it, 'The function of Government in this sphere is patron, not employer; in a sense, indeed, it is that of an impresario.'[45] Neither Hailsham himself nor the government was going to engage in organized planning for the future of pure science nor for the application of science to industry. The office of the Minister for Science was in any case not sufficiently staffed to tackle such a task: Hailsham himself remarked that he had no more than one busload of civil servants.

Within three years, it had become clear that the task was too much even for a Minister as competent and energetic as Hailsham. The Labour Party had been busy pushing out policy statements on the future of British science and technology.[46] Even a Conservative Party committee, under the chairmanship of Robert Carr, advocated a strong central Technical Policy Committee to oversee government science, although this was more radical than the government was prepared to concede and so did not become party policy.[47]

In March 1962, Macmillan appointed a Committee of Enquiry into the Organization of Civil Science, under the chairmanship of Sir Burke Trend, the Cabinet Secretary.[48] It is an oblique comment on the inadequacies of the Advisory Council on Scientific Policy that Macmillan had to go elsewhere to obtain such an investigation. The Trend Committee was to find that the structures put in place after the First World War, and the additions and accretions since the Second, no longer functioned properly. It was to propose instead sweeping reforms and a new dispensation that would properly manage the scientific enterprise for the national good. With the Trend enquiry, the administration of British science finally moved into the second half of the twentieth century.

Notes

1 See Martin Ryle, 'Radioastronomy: the Cambridge contribution', in *Search and Research* (Mullard Ltd, 1971).
2 Details of the subsidies given to the aircraft industry under Launch Aid can be found in successive issues of the Annual Review of Government Funded R&D (HMSO). Early in 1990, the government announced that yet more state aid would go to support the development of new aeroengines even though its avowed policy is not to support near-market or single company initiatives.
3 Keith Pavitt and Michael Worboys, *Science, Technology and the Modern Industrial State* (Butterworths, 1977).
4 A nice account of this and of the conflict between Lindemann and Tizard can be found in C. P. Snow, *Science and Government* (Harvard University Press, 1961).
5 Memorandum from Sir Henry Tizard quoted in J. B. Poole and K. Andrews, *The Government of Science in Britain* (Weidenfeld and Nicolson, 1972), p. 138.
6 Letter from Sir William Bragg to Admiral Lord Chatfield, Minister for Coordination of Defence, in Poole and Andrews, *Government of Science*, p. 140.
7 Snow, *Science and Government*, ch. 8.

8　*Science in War* (Penguin Special, 1940).
9　Solly Zuckerman, *Monkeys, Men and Missiles* (Collins, 1988) p. 273.
10　J. D. Bernal, *The Social Function of Science* (Routledge, 1939).
11　Gary Werskey, *The Visible College* (Allen Lane, 1978).
12　This was the description Max Perutz, the Nobel Prize-winning former director of the MRC's Cambridge Laboratory for Molecular Biology, used to describe the Advisory Board for the Research Councils' 'Strategy for the Science Base', see chapter 6.
13　Scientific Manpower, Report of a committee appointed by the Lord President of the Council under the chairmanship of Sir Alan Barlow, Cmd 6824, (HMSO, 1946).
14　Ian Varcoe, *Organising for Science in Britain* (OUP, 1974).
15　Association of Scientific Workers, *Science and the nation* (Penguin, 1947).
16　J. D. Bernal quoted in W. H. G. Armytage, *The Rise of the Technocrats* (Routledge and Kegan Paul, 1965).
17　Report of the Committee of Enquiry into the Organisation of Civil Science, under the Chairmanship of Sir Burke Trend (The Trend Report), Cmnd 2171 (HMSO, 1963).
18　Scientific Manpower (The Barlow Report) p. 8.
19　Zuckerman, *Monkeys, Men and Missiles*, p. 110.
20　First Annual Report of the Advisory Council on Science Policy Cmd 7465 (HMSO, 1948).
21　Zuckerman, *Monkeys, Men and Missiles*, p. 104.
22　Ibid., p. 108.
23　Hilary Rose and Steven Rose, *Science and Society* (Allen Lane 1969).
24　Nicholas Schoon, 'The Hovercraft: born 1959, dying 1989' *The Independent*, 29 May 1989, p. 15.
25　House of Commons Select Committee on Estimates, Third Report (1947).
26　Zuckerman, *Monkeys, Men and Missiles*, p. 105.
27　First Annual Report of the Advisory Council on Scientific Policy Cmd 7465, (HMSO, 1948).
28　Bernard Lovell, *The Story of Jodrell Bank* (OUP, 1968).
29　The Trend Report, p. 11.
30　The Future Organisation of the United Kingdom Atomic Energy Project, Cmd 8986 (HMSO, 1953) and the First Annual Report of the United Kingdom Atomic Energy Authority (HMSO, 1955).
31　Margaret Gowing (with Lorna Arnold), *Independence and Deterrence* (Macmillan, 1974).

32 Tom Wilkie, 'An energy policy in chaos' *The Independent*, 31 October 1988, p. 17.

33 Pavitt and Warboys, *Science, Technology*, pp. 62–3.

34 W. H. G. Armytage, *The Rise of the Technocrats* (Routledge and Kegan Paul, 1965).

35 Ibid., p. 209.

36 IBM, Annual Report for 1987. Note that IBM actually publishes figures for what it spends on research and development; even in the 1990s, few British companies do so and moves to make disclosure of R&D spending compulsory have made little headway.

37 J. G. Crowther, *The Cavendish Laboratory, 1874–1974* (Macmillan, 1974).

38 Fourth Annual Report of the UK Atomic Energy Authority (HMSO, 1959), Appendix I. National Institute for Research in Nuclear Science: First Annual Report for Year ended 31 March 1958.

39 Though it is now quite old, Robert Jungk's, *The Big Machine* (Andre Deutsch, 1969) is a lively and colourful introduction to the early days of CERN.

40 Speech by Professor W. Mitchell, Chairman of the Science and Engineering Research Council, to the Royal Society.

41 Department of Scientific and Industrial Research, Report of a Committee of Enquiry (The Jephcott Report), Cmd 9734 (HMSO, 1956).

42 *The Economist*, 22 August 1964, p. 70.

43 The Federation of British Industry *Civil Research Policy*, June 1963. *The Observer*, 20 September 1959.

44 *Hansard* vol. 681, col. 89–91, July 1963.

45 Viscount Hailsham, Eighth Fawley lecture, November 1961.

46 'Labour and the Scientific Revolution', policy statement at 1963 Annual conference.

47 'Science in Industry: the Influence of Government Policy', Conservative Political Centre (1962).

48 The Trend Report (1963).

5 The Age of Reform: the Trend Report, the Rothschild Report and the Sale of Science, 1963–1978

The recommendations of the Committee of Enquiry chaired by Sir Burke Trend transformed a system that had remained essentially unchanged for half a century. Yet only six years later, the system for the government support of civil research was changed yet again. This time the changes were ideologically motivated. Science was no longer seen as the engine of economic progress but rather as a commodity that could be bought off the shelf — no longer an investment but a cost, just another item of public expenditure for which due accounting had to be made.

The recommendations of the Trend Committee, published in October 1963, represented an administrative watershed.[1] They coincided with the reforms and expansion of higher education recommended by the Robbins Report,[2] and for the first time since the Great War, it looked as if the UK might truly equip itself as a modern industrial nation. In the end, there was a failure of nerve. But what came out of the Trend Committee was in a sense also a mark of continuity. No one doubted that science, properly organized, would deliver 'progress' — economic growth and prosperity. The prevalent belief was merely that the organization was deficient.

There was too a feeling that the education of the British had been in some way deficient and, as C.P. Snow put it, that the country had split into 'two cultures': one scientific, the other broadly literary/classical; and that the two were unable to communicate with each other.[3] Britain's relative economic decline stemmed in part, according to this analysis, from there being too few people in the higher reaches of most British companies trained in or with an understanding of the application of science to industry. The observation was by no means unique to Snow. In 1958, the year before Snow's lectures, Stephen Cotgrove had come to much the same conclusion in his study of technical education.[4] In particular, Cotgrove found the major factor in the slow growth of technical education was the apathetic and hostile 'attitude of industry towards the application of science to the production process'. The country's educational institutions had reinforced this attitude with their prejudice towards the ideals of a liberal education appropriate for a governing and administrative elite and against the changes that would be required to educate the scientific and technological elite needed by a successful industrial society. Similar observations have been made in our own time.[5]

But Snow also remarked that a cultural divide had developed within British science:

> most pure scientists have themselves been devastatingly ignorant of productive industry and many still are. Pure scientists and engineers often totally misunderstand each other. Pure scientists have by and large been dimwitted about engineers and applied science. Their instinct — perhaps sharpened in this country by the passion to find a new snobbism wherever possible, and to invent one if it doesn't exist — was to take it for granted that applied science was an occupation for second rate minds.[6]

Sir Peter Medawar remarked on the same fatal tendency to value the useless at the expense of the practical.[7] The theme was taken up politically: Aubrey Jones MP proposed in the House of Commons that a Ministry of Science and Technology be set up as a means of 'infusing technology with science and science with technology. The problem of science in this country is the bias in the social system.'[8]

Nevertheless, in the early 1960s, there was confidence that such faults were curable. A different attitude was to come at the beginning of the next decade, when doubt set in as to whether there was any economic return to be gained from giving scientists large amounts of the taxpayers' money and letting them get on with what they thought were the interesting problems.

The Trend Committee found two general deficiencies with the civil research system as it had grown up since the war.[9] The first was that 'the agencies concerned with the promotion of civil science do not in the aggregate constitute a coherent and articulated pattern of organisation.' The second problem was that 'the arrangements for co-ordinating Government's scientific effort and for apportioning the available resources between the agencies on a rational basis are insufficiently clear and precise.' The institutions that had grown up did not provide a comprehensive and systematic coverage of the field of civil science as a whole, the Committee continued:

> The research councils created to promote research in medicine and agriculture have stood the test of time; but in the case of the newer developments no similarly coherent arrangements exist. In both nuclear physics and space research responsibility is dispersed among various bodies ... Arrangements which had a sound historical origin no longer appear to correspond with the needs of the modern situation. The most striking example is perhaps the Admiralty's continuing responsibility for the Royal Observatory, despite the fact that responsibility for other forms of research in astronomy rests with DSIR.

But it was the role of the government in promoting industrial research and development, and the role of the DSIR in particular, that exercised the Committee. It criticized the 'lack of adequate arrangements for co-ordinating the activities of DSIR and those of other authorities concerned with promoting research and development in particular fields of industrial enterprise'.

The Trend Committee broadly endorsed the work and structure of the Medical and Agricultural Research Councils. It also endorsed the 'dual-support system' for the financing of research in the universities. In a comment that has relevance to the 1990s, the committee remarked that 'it is important that there should be more than one source of funds for research; centralised provision carries with it the serious risk that potentially fruitful ideas may be nipped in the cold winds of chance or academic prejudice.' The Committee came down against the research councils taking over responsibility for funding all research in the universities.

The Committee's most important recommendation was to wind up the Department of Scientific and Industrial Research. In its place, there were to be three research councils administratively similar to the medical and agricultural research councils.

The Science Research Council was to take over responsibility for supporting the relevant research in universities and similar institutions, and for postgraduate awards in science and technology. The functions of NIRNS would be transferred from the Atomic Energy Authority into the physics and mathematics division of the proposed new council. That division would also be responsible for the scientific aspects of Britain's membership of CERN. Similarly, the responsibility for space research, including relations with ESRO, would be transferred to the council's astronomy and space science division which would assume direct control of the Royal Observatory. Thus all aspects of astronomy would come under one research council for the first time. The Committee, however, rejected suggestions that the Meteorological Office be transferred from the Air Ministry to the council.

The second innovation was the proposed creation of a Natural Resources Research Council. This essentially was the Nature Conservancy with a much expanded research arm. The proposed council would retain the Conservancy's responsibilities for managing nature reserves, but in addition would conduct research into hydrology, fisheries and related aspects of aquatic biology, oceanography, forestry, and would also take over the British Geological Survey and the Soil Survey. In the end, the proposed demarcations did not work efficiently. The organization came into being as the Natural Environment Research

Council, rather than Natural Resources. And some eight years later, in July 1972, the management of nature reserves was hived off altogether into a reconstituted Nature Conservancy Council, while the research functions were carried on by the Natural Environment Research Council (NERC). NERC was assigned much of the Development Commission's research work. In addition, the Trend Committee recommended abolishing the Overseas Research Council.

In the field of industrially applicable research, the Trend Committee proposed a completely new organization: the Industrial Research and Development Authority (IRDA). The Authority was to stand in the same relationship to the Minister of Science as the other research councils but, the Committee felt, it should not simply be a research council: 'If research and development are to make an effective contribution to industrial growth, the responsible agency must be more executive in nature than a Research Council.'

The IRDA was to take over the rump of the DSIR. Moreover, the Trend Committee proposed that it should take over the National Research Development Corporation also. It should, however, be relieved of the statutory limitation on the existing NRDC to break even overall. One final aspect of the IRDA's work was that it should act as a procurement agency on behalf of other departments, placing development contracts with industry.

Significantly, the Trend Report was silent about the Atomic Energy Authority and the Ministry of Aviation, the two most important spenders on industrial research and development. Furthermore, rather than marrying pure science more closely with industrial applied research and so correcting the deficiencies apparent to Snow and others, the Committee's scheme of things threatened to reinforce the division between pure and applied research by hiving off the research councils into a sub-branch of the Ministry of Education, distancing them administratively from the IRDA.

The Trend Report was vigorously criticized for not going far enough. In a House of Lords debate in March 1964, Lord Bowden dismissed the report as 'fundamentally unimportant;

even, one might say, irrelevant'.[10] He criticized the way in which:

> it ignored the very complex questions which are posed by the Ministry of Defence, the Atomic Energy Authority and by those large research establishments controlled by the nationalised industries. The prosperity of British industry and the achievement of better designs which can be manufactured and sold at a profit, should have been the primary concern of any Committee concerned with research and development. The fact that this was not mentioned seems sufficient condemnation at least of the terms of reference with which the committee was burdened.

The Economist and *The Spectator* joined the chorus of criticism. *The Economist* put its finger on the deficiencies of separating pure from applied science and advocated a central Ministry of Science whose remit would also include the moneys spent by the Atomic Energy Authority and the Aviation Ministry.[11] *The Spectator* had a different angle, however, and its criticism was remarkably percipient.[12] It questioned the Trend Committee's acceptance of the Haldane principle that scientists should be given money and then allowed to get on with science: this was 'a principle of Government by good luck (which may well turn out to be bad luck)'. In its place, *The Spectator* argued that government departments should be more *dirigiste* in commissioning research — a proposal that was to be given concrete form within a few years by Lord Rothschild's reforms.

The Trend Committee's proposal to set up an Industrial Research Development Authority was not enacted. By the time the Trend Committee reported, Britain was on the verge of a General Election and one in which, for the first and last time, science was to be a major issue. Despite the fact that Macmillan's record showed him to be the first British Prime Minister for half a century interested in matters of science and technology policy, it was the Labour opposition that gained the initiative on this issue. In October 1963, Harold Wilson told the Labour Party Conference 'We are redefining and we are restating our socialism in terms of the scientific revolution ... the Britain that is going to be forged in the white heat of this revolution will be no place for restrictive practices or outdated methods on either side of industry.'[13]

The rhetoric owed a lot to Bernal and the science and socialism programme of the 1930s, but the reality was rather disappointing. When Wilson was elected to power in 1964, his government translated most of the Trend Committee's proposals into action. But the proposed IRDA never saw the light of day. Instead, the Labour government set up the Ministry of Technology to fulfil the same functions. The decision had the unfortunate effect of splitting pure science away from applied and institutionalizing that split in the very structure of government. The research councils became a minor part of the responsibilities of the Secretary of State for Education and Science. In fact, the responsibility has always been delegated to a junior minister, effectively depriving civil science of any representative at Cabinet level. The irony of the Trend/Wilson reforms, which were intended to strengthen the position of science and technology in government, is that they effectively devalued them in political terms. The political standing of pure science fell earlier than that of industrial or applied science. The Trend Committee had recommended that its proposed IRDA should stand to ministers in the same fashion as the research councils, i.e. the researchers should be isolated from direct political control by the interpolation of an autonomous research-council like body. Instead, applied or industrially related science became the direct responsibility of the Minister of Technology at Cabinet level.

A further consequence of the reorganization was that, for all the Wilsonian rhetoric about science at the heart of his administration, for the first time since the war there was no overall central apparatus for providing the government with advice on science and technology. The Wilson government had followed Trend in abolishing the old Advisory Council on Scientific Policy. It was replaced with a similarly sounding Council for Scientific Policy (CSP). But this body existed only to advise the Secretary of State for Education and Science, not the government as a whole, and the CSP's remit covered only academic science funded by the research councils and largely performed in universities or research institutes. An Advisory Council for Technology was set up to assist the new Minister for Technology. Unlike the CSP, the technology committee never reported publicly. Within a couple of years, the loss of advice at the centre had become obvious and yet another advisory body was brought into existence, the Central Advisory Council for Science and Technology, under the chairmanship of the Chief Scientific Adviser to the government, Solly Zuckerman.

The most radical creation of the Wilson years was, of course, the Ministry of Technology. It was a small organization originally, with responsibility for four industries: computers, electronics, telecommunications, and machine tools. Shortly thereafter it acquired mechanical and electrical engineering and motor vehicles from the Board of Trade and then, in February 1967, it got the aeronautical industry when the Ministry of Aviation was finally wound up. The Ministry had two functions: one was to promote industrial efficiency; the other to promote the use of new technology in industry. When the young and energetic Anthony Wedgwood Benn became Minister, the thrust of the department changed and the promotion of advanced technology in industry began to take second place to large-scale intervention in industry itself. For the first time since the creation of British Dyestuffs in 1914, a British government decided that the country's industrial competitiveness required more than just exhortation and collaborative research and development projects. Through the Industrial Reorganization Corporation (IRC), the Wilson administration began to restructure (private) industry in Britain. The first target was the computer industry. In 1954, the first industrial computer in the world had been installed in the offices of a British company: LEO, the Lyons Electronic Office, had been produced in Britain for the catering firm of Lyons to do its accounts. But leadership had passed to the Americans and in particular to IBM. In the spring of 1968, the Ministry of Technology forced the amalgamation of civil computer manufacture in Britain into one large company International Computers Ltd (ICL). Similarly, the IRC played a leading role in the merger between the General Electric

Company and Associated Electrical Industries. There was also a complex series of manoeuvres concerning the ownership of the Cambridge Instrument Company.

In the end, the brief experiment of 'Mintech' and the IRC was not to be any more conspicuously successful in regenerating British industry than its predecessors. Rather than the promoter of industrial efficiency, the IRC inevitably became an instrument of government involvement in industry.[14] And the enterprises that were the subject of so much fevered attention in the 1960s do not appear as shining beacons of British industry in the 1990s. GEC is an industrial dinosaur grown fat on the easy money of defence contracts. ICL no longer exists as an independent company, having first been taken over by STC and then sold on to the Japanese company Fujitsu. Writing from the perspective of the 1970s, Pavitt and Worboys noted:

> Despite these apparent changes, the main problems are still unsolved today. The Government remains heavily committed to large-scale Government-financed programmes of R&D related to defence, civil aviation and nuclear energy. The powerful vested interests remain, protected by growing nationalism, and a cloak of government secrecy greater than in any other supposed liberal democracy. At the same time there is the continuing technological backwardness of British industry. In spite of the brave talk of the technological revolution, Britain's relative productivity and world export share in manufactured goods has continued to decline in the 1970s. Industry financed R&D is much lower than in West Germany and Japan; and engineering goods are of inferior technical quality. School leavers are reluctant to go into science and, even more so, into engineering. Even when they do they are still reluctant to go to work in industry. After two World Wars and years of protected Empire markets, British industry finds itself in the same position as at the beginning of this century: industrially and technically inferior to Germany and the USA, with the difference now that Japan and France will soon join them.[15]

Towards the end of the decade, Mr Benn's department floated the idea of an industrial research and development organization — a centralized contract R&D agency.[16] This statutory corporation, the British Research and Development Corporation, would subsume within it all the government departmental R&D establishments (including parts of the UK Atomic Energy Authority, but excluding defence work). The idea was that customers, whether government or private industry, would pay fees to have 'contract science' performed by the corporation. The proposal, which contained the germ of the 'customer—contractor principle', was set out in a Green Paper in 1970, but came to nothing as the Labour Party was voted out of office. However, the customer—contractor principle was to be the centre piece of science policy in the administration that followed.

The proposals of the Trend Committee, as amended by the Labour government, set the pattern for the organization of government science ever since. In the 1990s, we are further from the time of the Trend Committee than it was from the structures instituted at the end of the war, but even though civil science in Britain has experienced more stress over the past quarter-century than it experienced in the years up to Trend, the institutions have remained. The majority of 'pure' scientists practising today will have had little knowledge of anything other than the Science Research Council and its sister organizations; most of those who embarked on an industrial research career will have been supported through their doctoral 'training in research methods' by one of the councils and will know nothing of the now defunct Department of Scientific and Industrial Research.

But just as the period of the Trend Committee formed the present-day structures of civil science, so the foundations of its future problems can now, with the benefit of hindsight, be discerned from that period. The amount of money the state spent on civil research and development was growing fast: at its maximum rate in 1966—7, the science budget had grown by 13 per cent per annum. By the end of the 1960s, that had slowed to an annual growth of 4.5 per cent, with the prospect of declining to a still smaller figure.[17]

Enormous though that increase was by today's standards,

budgetary limitations had already caused some pain. In 1967, the Council for Scientific Policy had advocated that the UK participate in building the proposed 300 GeV particle accelerator, a successor to the highly successful device that had been built and operated by CERN, the European laboratory for particle physics, just outside Geneva. This advice was rejected, and Britain declined to participate, because the project would have taken too much money from 'domestic' science. In the end, the 300GeV machine was rethought and its cost reduced by siting it next to the existing machine at CERN and the UK belatedly and reluctantly rejoined the project. But the incident was a harbinger of much worse to come when the costly reality of international science had to be faced in the 1980s.

By the late 1960s, the Science Research Council was talking in terms of 'Selectivity and Concentration in the Support of Research' and in a report of that name published in 1970 made it clear that the council would support certain university departments on the basis of their research leadership and, by the same token, reduce the money going to other programme areas or researchers that had lost impetus.[18] This too would become a dominant theme in the 1980s.

When Edward Heath took office in 1970, he was committed to reorganizing the machinery of central government. In the area of civil research and development, this review and reorganization produced two landmark reports, which have essentially dominated British science ever since. Lord Rothschild, head of the Central Policy Review Staff and a former chairman of the Agricultural Research Council, investigated and reported on 'The Organisation and Management of Government R&D'. In parallel, Sir Frederick, now Lord, Dainton, the chairman of the Council for Scientific Policy reported on 'The Future of the Research Council System' to the then Secretary of State for Education and Science, Margaret Thatcher.[19]

Of the two, the Dainton Report was better researched and more elegantly written: it had much less influence on subsequent events. The report was prompted initially by an attempt by the Ministry of Agriculture, Fisheries and Food to hijack the Agricultural Research Council. An interdepartmental committee of civil servants, headed by a Mr S.P. Osmond of the Civil Service Department, advocated the transfer in 1970. This threatened breach of the Haldane principle that research councils should be independent of administrative departments of state was effectively seen off, although MAFF was soon to gain a considerable say in the running of agricultural research through the execution of the Rothschild proposals. The second stimulus to Dainton's report was the realization that the period of exponential growth in the government's civil science budget was over.

In the main, the Dainton Report was concerned with the sort of science that the government funded as a 'public good' – the academic work that would not necessarily yield patentable products, but that was the necessary foundation for the applied research carried out either by administrative departments for their own purposes or by industry for economic gain. In administrative terms, this was the research funded by the Department of Education's science budget and, as such, the report's subject matter represented, in monetary terms, less than half of government-supported civil R&D. Much of the discussion of British science policy since the mid-1960s has been confused by a failure to distinguish which part of civil research and development is being referred to: a clear distinction has to be made, but often is not, between the Department of Education's science budget and the total amount spent by government on research and development, which includes spending in industrial laboratories, on applied science for administrative purposes, as well as the 'science budget'. The confusion makes it easy for unscrupulous politicians to claim that, when in office, their party has increased the budget for science while omitting to mention more than compensating decreases elsewhere in the government structure.

The Dainton Report highlighted the difficulties that would be created for academic research by the lower rate of growth in the science budget. Such difficulties would be exacerbated by the increasing 'sophistication factor' (meaning that it becomes more expensive to make equivalent advances in knowledge) and by the growth of 'big science' (where the threshold of expenditure needed to achieve any worthwhile result tends to rise continually, as in particle physics). As a result, it would cost more tomorrow to obtain the same amount of 'good science' as today. The 300GeV particle accelerator project proposed by the European Laboratory for Particle Physics in the late 1960s was a perfect example of both tendencies. These developments could be partly offset, the Dainton Committee believed, by increased international collaboration and by increased selectivity in the support of science. Both themes were to dominate policy towards basic research a decade later.

The Dainton Committee's principal recommendation was that a Board for the Research Councils be established, on the same statutory footing as the research councils themselves, responsible to the Secretary of State for Education and Science. It would be responsible for financial allocation to individual research councils.

In the event, the proposal was not carried through. The Secretary of State appointed an Advisory Board for the Research Councils, which lacked the status of having a Royal Charter as possessed by the research councils themselves. It was a solution which had the political advantage of not requiring parliamentary time for legislation that would have been required to grant the Board a charter. However, two decades after Dainton's report, the relative weakness of the Advisory Board compared to the research councils themselves became once again a serious issue of national policy towards basic science, at a time when a rational sharing of diminished public funds was imperative.[20] Dainton did however venture into the arena of the research sponsored by government departments to suggest that the statutory Board for the Research Councils could oversee the provision of scientific support to administrative departments. The proposal was rejected. The Rothschild Report stated flatly that the administrative departments, 'do not require scientific support, but applied R&D, to achieve specific predetermined objectives'.

Lord Rothschild's report reflected the beginning of the managerial period of government's attitude to science and the abandonment of the Haldane principle, hence the significant appearance of the word 'management' in its title. The differences in approach, in tone, and in content between Lord Rothschild's report and the Trend Committee's report six years earlier are striking. The Trend Committee analysed the institutions that then existed for the government support of civil science and reviewed their history, thus setting its recommendations in the context of the natural organic development of these bodies. Moreover, for all the criticism that the Trend Committee had concentrated too much upon academic science and had done too little to tackle the problems of science as applied to British industry, the Rothschild dispensation, which was supposed to cover all science, also focused rather heavily on academic science. As the Science Research Council was to observe acidly, in a report supposed to be covering all areas of government R&D there was disproportionate attention to the science budget of the Department of Education and Science. The relationship between government-funded science and industrial innovation was simply not addressed.

The Rothschild recommendations were ideological and destructive. The study contained little in the way of argument, and much that was simply assertion. The report was an abstract piece of analysis which took little account of the actual institutions and of the inconsistencies and overlaps that are inevitable to the execution of any policy. Instead, the Rothschild Report proposed a blueprint for the administration of science, but the design was of almost baroque intricacy and of a rigidity that meant the whole scheme was in difficulty if any part of the design was not executed properly. Moreover, its proper execution would have instituted a new tier of bureaucracy in the administration of science. Scarcely a decade after Lord Hailsham had been content with but a busload of bureaucrats, Lord Rothschild would have had them by the trainload.

The Rothschild proposals had three basic elements: the customer—contractor principle should operate on applied research; the administrative departments should expand their chief scientists' organizations in order that they could act as informed customers when they bought a piece of research; and a substantial proportion of the block grant going to the Medical, Agricultural, and Natural Environment Research Councils should be removed from them; henceforth they would have to win that money by competing against other organizations to obtain research contracts placed by the customer departments. The Medical and Agricultural Research Councils were precisely the ones with which the Trend Committee could find virtually no fault and which were left untouched by its reforms. Why the situation should have changed so drastically within the short space of six years was a question that Lord Rothschild's analysis left unanswered.

Rothschild started by dismissing as unanswerable or meaningless, most of the questions that successive governments had grappled with since the First World War. There was no way of knowing, he said, whether the UK was doing too much, too little or about the right amount of R&D. Nor was there even any point in trying to assess how much R&D the government was doing: 'it is doubtful whether any central body can or should try critically to evaluate the Government's R&D as a whole.' Moreover, he asserted, there could not be a correct balance between the resources devoted to pure and to applied research, the question was meaningless. Three other central questions at the heart of successive governments' science policies he dismissed as irrelevances that would sort themselves out once his logical and efficient system for the organization and management of R&D had been put in place: there was therefore no point in asking what R&D the government was doing that should not be done; nor what should be done that was being left undone; nor whether the R&D should be done more intramurally or extra-murally.

Pace Lord Rothschild, these questions have persisted. Indeed, in the 1980s, the difficulties experienced by the 'logical, flexible, humane and decentralised, efficient system' that he set up have made these questions more not less insistent. Since 1983, the Science and Technology Secretariat in the Cabinet Office has been doing precisely what Lord Rothschild dismissed as impossible: critically evaluating the government's R&D as a whole. These annual reviews have highlighted gross disparities in the overall pattern of spending, areas of necessary research that were not being done, and unnecessary research that had not been terminated. During the early 1970s, the budget for basic scientific research carried out by the research councils fell sharply, picked up again a little, and then oscillated unpredictably. In the 1980s, the research councils' budget grew in real terms but the overall moneys available for curiosity-driven research fell because of a sharp cut in funding for science in the universities themselves. These complicated budgetary problems raised all the more acutely questions about the total amount of R&D the country performed and the balance of spending between pure and applied research.

The key guiding principle of Lord Rothschild's review was 'that applied R&D, that is R&D with a practical application as its objective must be done on a customer contractor basis. The customer says what he wants; the contractor does it (if he can); and the customer pays.' It was an idea of blinding simplicity and apparent elegance. Yet there was not one word of justification in the report, nor an analysis of how (or even if) the previous arrangements had failed. And the elegance of the idea soon got lost when Lord Rothschild confronted the complexities of the real situation with which the government had to deal.

The customer–contractor principle was intended to apply not only to research that an administrative department commissioned from an outside agency, but also to intra-mural research commissioned from the department's own laboratories. Thus, within a single department, Lord Rothschild envisaged setting up one individual, the chief scientist, with a large supporting organization to act as the informed customer, and another individual, the controller R&D, with another organization, to offer research sevices and so act as the contractor. When the research councils competed for contracts from the administrative departments, the secretary or chairman of the Council was supposed to act in the role of controller R&D.

Lord Rothschild dismissed as impossible the idea of striking a balance between pure and applied research and he also had a clear view of how to distinguish applied from pure or basic research: almost by definition, applied research was a piece of scientific work for which there existed a customer willing to pay to have it carried out and to receive the results. None the less, he found it impossible to keep the demarcation clear, and made provision for a 10 per cent 'General Research Surcharge'. He wrote 'Virtually all applied R&D laboratories sooner or later engage, overtly or clandestinely, in research which is not directly concerned with the programmes commissioned by the customers: and it is a good thing that they do.' Controllers of R&D were to be allowed to levy a 10 per cent surcharge on the research contracts they administered to support this general research. Rothchild was anxious that this element be quantified and made explicit in contracts, but he gave no reasons for arriving at a figure of 10 per cent. As events turned out, it proved impossible for the contractors to squeeze that 10 per cent out of their customers who saw no reason to pay for research that they had not commissioned.

The Rothschild reorganization explicitly breached the Haldane principle that research should be carried out by bodies which were not directly dependent on the favour of ministers or senior civil servants in the administrative departments. Haldane had recommended a structure for the support of research that 'places responsibility to Parliament in the hands of a Minister who is ... immune from any suspicion of being biased by administrative considerations against the application of the results of research'.[21] Rothschild, in part, dismisses the very notion of there actually being a 'Haldane principle' (the report makes eloquent use of quotation marks typographically to deny the concept legitimacy) and then airily discounts it as out of date: 'The "Haldane Principle" has evidently little or no bearing on the conduct and management of Government R&D in the '70s.'

Those ministers who were actively involved with 'administrative considerations', or at least their chief scientists, were to be the very people who should determine what research should be done, 'to achieve specific predetermined objectives', according to Rothschild. But although this conclusion might have been defensible when focusing specifically on applied research and development, Lord Rothschild broadened the concept to include the work of the research councils. The autonomy that they had in respect of the scientific content of their programmes repesented 'an unsatisfactory situation in some cases' Rothschild aid. 'However distinguished, intelligent and practical scientists nay be, they cannot be so well qualified to decide what the needs of the nation are, as those responsible for ensuring that hose needs are met.'

The Rothschild Report opened the way for closer ties between cientists and their political paymasters. The clearest recent nstance of this came in 1982, when the chairman of the Natural Environment Research Council and of the Advisory Board for the Research Council were summoned to Downing St to explain why they had decided to cut funding to the British Antarctic Survey. Whatever the scientific merits of the ase, the Survey's activities gave Britain a legitimate presence n Antarctica and in the south Atlantic, the scene of the Falklands War. Funding was restored and since then, the Advisory Board or the Research Councils has explicitly recognized the political dimension to some scientific questions, such as Britain's continued membership of the European Particle Physics Laboratory, CERN, near Geneva, or the fate of the British Geological Survey.[22]

It is not clear that the nation has obtained significantly better cience in the two decades since Rothschild reported than it had got in the preceding half-century. In the event, 'those esponsible for meeting the needs of the nation' proved incompetent commissioners of science and careless stewards of what had been entrusted to them. The chief scientist organizations never acquired the power, influence and command of the budget that would have been required for the system to unction properly. The 10 per cent research surcharge was a dead letter almost from the start. And when rampant inflation hit in the mid-1970s, research budgets did not keep pace, and n the consequent reigning-in of public expenditure, research was one of the first items to be cut.

Rothschild's proposals got an almost uniformly hostile reeption from the scientific community.[23] The Royal Society elt that it 'presents a drab and uninspiring future which will not attract young men into science and which will lower the quality of the work done by older men already committed to a scientific career'. (Apparently the Royal Society then believed that there was no such thing as a woman scientist.) The Science Research Council, as previously mentioned, decried the too heavy emphasis on the science budget of the Department of Education and Science.

The Commons Select Committee on Science and Technology observed that 'many scientists felt particularly threatened by the proposals and were offended by comments relating to the pay of chairmen and members of research councils.' The Council for Scientific Policy, the Royal Society and the three research councils most affected by the Rothschild proposals all complained that he had not consulted them adequately before producing his report and they did not feel that some of his assertions could be based on their evidence 'and they had looked in vain for alternative supporting evidence'. The Select Committee concluded 'that the atmosphere of uncertainty of the past few years combined with frequent reviews of organisation were affecting the morale of research workers.' Complaints of diminishing morale were to be repeated in subsequent years

One of the few exceptions to all this criticism was Professor Sir Herman Bondi, former chief scientist at the Ministry of Defence, and later Chairman of the Natural Environment Research Council. Shortly after the proposals had come into force, Bondi wrote in support of the customer–contractor principle, 'In our MOD ... it has been firmly established that when you give a contract to a manufacturer to develop and build a particular missile for you, that contract has two outputs. One is the missile you have contracted for, but the other is a contractor who knows how to build missiles.'[24] No one seems to have remarked on the peculiarity of the Ministry of Defence's procurement policy: that it placed contracts with companies that it acknowledged did not know how to make the required product. On the operation of the Rothschild principle, Professor Bondi was sanguine: 'If you get shortsighted customers, then they tend to engage in what I refer to as intellectual asset stripping. I am very anxious naturally to push our customer [i.e. government departments contracting for research with NERC which Bondi at that time headed] in the direction of building up our strength, because it is in their interest so to spend the taxpayers' money today that more value comes out of it tomorrow.' Before the end of the decade, a review of the Rothschild system in operation reported that while the research association were able routinely to add a surcharge to their contracts with the Department of Industry to cover the general research that Rothschild praised, NERC (another contractor used by the Department of Industry) had not been able to negotiate a surcharge. Alas, it was intellectual asset-stripping that prevailed.

The practical weapon that Rothschild had given the administrative departments was a proposal to claw back large proportions of the science vote income of the Medical, Agricultural, and Natural Environment Research Councils to the commissioning departments. In 1971–2 these three research councils received a total of £56.4 million from the science budget of the Department of Education and Science. The government proposed a gradual reduction over a period of four years so that, in 1975–6, £20 million would have been transferred from the science budget to the customer departments. The ARC was to suffer most heavily, losing £10 million in 1975–6 from a budget that had stood at only £18.7 million in 1971–2. The cut in the MRC budget was less than a quarter, while that of the NERC was around a third. It is worth noting that almost all the changes effected were executed by means of government policy and budgeting changes. As in the case of the formation of the Advisory Board for the Research Councils, the Rothschild proposals needed no primary legislation to give them effect.

Given Lord Rothschild's strictures about the impossibility of coordinating science policy centrally, the post of chief scientific advisor to the government seemed unnecessary and when the then advisor, Sir Alan Cottrell, retired from his post in 1974, he was not replaced. But by 1976, the expected results were not flowing from the new system and so the government again reviewed the arrangements that existed for coordination of its research activities. A new advisory body was formed, incorporating sources of advice external to the government, the Advisory Council for Applied Research and Development. A coordinating

committee of departmental chief scientists and permanent secretaries was set up, and a chief scientist, John Ashworth, was
appointed to the Central Policy Review Staff.[25]

In March 1979, a major review of the effects of the Rothschild
system on the research councils was carried out.[26] The review
gave the impression that the new system was working reasonably
well. But one research council was not happy. The Medical
Research Council was vehemently opposed to the introduction
of a customer—contractor relationship between itself and the
Department of Health and Social Security. More correctly, it
was not the customer—contractor principle that was objection-
able so much as the idea that money should be taken away
from the science vote.[27] The Secretary to the MRC at the
time, Sir James Gowans, has expressed support for the customer—contractor principle but only so long as it was on top of
the pre-existing core programme of research.

The health departments were in any case unable to put
forward new ideas for research on the scale that the Rothschild
system provided for. Up to 1976, the MRC negotiated 142
'notional' commissions with the health departments — all of
them derived from the Council's existing core programme of
research. Only one specific new commission was negotiated.
By 1977–8 the proportion of the MRC's budget coming from
health department commissions had fallen, leaving the council
some £900,000 short of its expected appropriation. Lord
Rothschild's 'efficient' system for commissioning research failed
at the first unforeseen obstacle: the rampant inflation that beset
the British economy during the 1970s. By 1981, the Secretary
of the MRC had succeeded in persuading the health departments, and the House of Commons public accounts committee
that the system was unworkable. The customer—contractor
arrangement was abandoned and the MRC won back control
over that part of its budget that had previously been earmarked
for DHSS contracts.

The two other research councils did not exert themselves as
energetically as Sir James Gowans to regain their moneys;
indeed, as noted above, the chairman of the NERC was a
positive enthusiast for the Rothschild reforms. They were thus

in a much more exposed position when financial stringency really began to bite. It is perhaps no coincidence that, by the late 1980s, the future of the Agricultural and the Natural Environment Research Councils had been put in some doubt.[28] The idea of a merger of the two councils has now been abandoned. Not least of the factors inhibiting reorganization in the late 1980s was again the reluctance of government to legislate.

With three of the research councils dependent for a substantial fraction of their income on the vagaries of research contracts from the administrative departments, core funding from the science budget of the Department of Education became that much more important for the well-being of 'pure' science and the morale of its practitioners. The rate of increase in the science budget had peaked in 1966–7, but was still running at about 4 per cent in 1972–3. But when the government of Edward Heath announced reductions in public expenditure in 1973, growth in the budget for basic science was replaced by decline in 1974–6.

Further cuts were announced by the Wilson government in 1976, affecting the years up to 1979. It was not a monotonic decline: in 1978, the then Secretary of State for Education and Science, Mrs Shirley Williams, produced some extra money for equipment. But the reductions in the science budget coincided with the collapse of the quinquennial system for financing university administration.[29] As early as 1973, a year before the quinquennial system gave way, the University Grants Committee had written to universities to say that it had no funds to increase science places (other than in medicine). And so, less than a decade after Robbins and the Trend reforms, the brake was put on any further increase in the numbers of scientists being trained in the UK. The country's attempt to educate more of its citizens and equip them with the skills necessary to run an industrial society in the final quarter of the twentieth century had come to an end.

By 1975, the UGC had told Cambridge University that it could not have a new science building because of excess provision of science facilities elsewhere. Worse was to come: between

1973 and 1979, the number of home research students in science fell by 10 per cent. The end of the quinquennial system was also the beginning of the end of the dual support system for research carried out in British universities. Between 1973 and 1979, the number of laboratory technicians declined by 5 per cent, and the amount of money university departments spent on consumables and other support fell by 19 per cent.

Throughout the 1970s, the Advisory Board for the Research Councils tried to cope with the rise of 'big science' against a background of falling budgets for basic research.[30] It consciously intervened to shift the pattern of funding away from 'big science'. The Science Research Council's domestic expenditure on high-energy physics and on space sciences fell by a third in real terms between 1973–4 and 1977–8. The two UK accelerators, Nina and Nimrod, were closed, and experimental work concentrated on international laboratories – principally CERN, but to some extent the German DESY electron accelerator near Hamburg. (It is a telling contrast in the positions of the two nations that the Germans were able to build a domestic laboratory that became an international facility operating at the forefront of particle physics, just at the time that the British were closing their machines.) But the commitment to participating in international organizations which, at the start of the decade had appeared to be an inexpensive way of remaining at the forefront of 'big science', had turned into a liability. By 1978–9, more than 16 per cent of the total budget for basic science was taken up by international commitments. Internationalism was the chosen solution in space science also, when the last remnant of Britain's pretensions to an independent space research programme vanished with the abandonment of the Skylark rocket project.

The subsequent fate of the two domestic high-energy physics machines illuminates some of the problems of managing research in a time of limited budgets and expensive central facilities. Nina was cannibalized and turned into a giant X-ray machine. Electron accelerators of this type naturally generate copious quantities of 'synchrotron' radiation: intense beams of X-rays that come off as the electrons travel in their circular path round the ring. For the purposes of high-energy physics, this radiation represents an energy loss and a constraint on how much the particles can be accelerated. But since at least 1913, there has been a strong tradition in British science of using X-rays to probe the structure of crystals and the arrangement of atoms in other solid materials. Deciphering the double helix of DNA could not have been done without the X-ray crystallography work of Rosalind Franklin at Kings College, London, and the work on the structure of haemoglobin and myoglobin also depended on X-ray crystallography. Bragg, Bernal and Dorothy Hodgkin all developed and applied the technique. Thus, when the focus of work at the Daresbury Laboratory was switched from high-energy physics to synchrotron radiation, there was a large community of users already in existence able and willing to take immediate advantage of the advanced X-ray facilities.

Nimrod, on the other hand, was cannibalized and became a pulsed neutron source, now known as ISIS. This is a different and more exotic tool for investigating the atomic structure of materials. No large community of prospective users existed to take advantage of the new facility. Instead, it would appear that the decision to convert Nimrod was taken at least as much to preserve some sort of *raison d'être* for the Rutherford laboratory where it was situated, and to find some occupation for its large staff. Some commentators have seen this as a failure of management nerve by the Science Research Council in the 1970s, and it certainly shows how the existence of large central organizations can influence science policy and the direction of research through simple institutional self-preservation. The existence of the machine has determined the science that is being done, rather than scientists deciding what is likely to be most productive and interesting research. *Ex post facto*, a user community has been gradually built up to take advantage of the facility but, although ISIS has absorbed a great deal of the SERC's resources, by 1990 it was still a larger facility than could be justified by the UK user community. Now that the machine exists, the SERC is trying with some success to attract interest in it from non-British users — a sort of *post hoc* internationalization, which is not the best way of going about funding large facilities.

Moreover, there is now a danger that having called these domestic users into existence, ISIS is beginning to get old in its turn. Thus pressures may build up for a replacement. The episode must leave open several questions about whether the best science was obtained for the money that has been spent, and whether the Science Research Council in the 1970s ought not to have had a clearer idea of how it intended to develop the future of the sciences that it funded.

The 1970s marked a shift towards more applied research, even for work financed from the science vote. There was a 15 per cent rise in the money for the Science Research Council's engineering activities over three years. Special programmes in polymer engineering, marine technology and production engineering were started up.

By 1979, things had begun to get nasty. The Advisory Board for the Research Councils reported that the previous few years had been 'a difficult period for British science'. The first problem was 'the combined effect on the science budget of the Government's restraint on public expenditure and of a high rate of inflation', while the second was the difficulty of adjusting to the Rothschild system. As Britain struggled through the in-famous 'winter of discontent', the Advisory Board pleaded with the government 'that a period of sustained real growth in expenditure at a minimum rate of 4% per annum is essential'.[31]

If extra money was not forthcoming, then, the Board warned, crucial items of research in astronomy, high-energy physics and space research would have to be abandoned. 'Big science is reaching a point at which we run the risk of losing a valuable national competence.' This would deleteriously affect British industry, it argued, because those subjects are based upon the most advanced technologies, and British industry would lose the chance of gaining experience in these technologies and would accordingly be less well placed to succeed in the highly competitive international market for high-technology products.

Moreover, increasing numbers of applications for grants to support research were having to be refused, even though the applications were judged to be worth supporting. 'The country has thus been unable to make proper use of the talents of the available manpower or to offer the right opportunities to attract good young scientists into research with the result that an important part of a whole generation has been lost to research.'[32]

The Board concluded with a spirited defence of the rationale for government support of basic scientific research:

> We cannot reduce our effort in basic research in the expectation that we can simply apply the results of work done in other countries. Although the results of fundamental research are usually freely available in the end, only a broadly based and flourishing national research community, in the thick of the international effort to advance scientific knowledge can keep abreast of the work of their collaborators and competitors abroad and assess its significance. Second, many of our problems are specific to ourselves and so the relevant work is not done elsewhere and there can be no guarantee that we can rely on the efforts of others to provide the fundamental research results which our own applied scientists and technologists will need in the future. Finally, the country which originates the best ideas should have a head start over its competitors in developing and marketing them and in enjoying the consequent economic and social benefits.[33]

It would be rash to assert that Britain could afford to withdraw from important areas of science on the grounds that they did not appear to have economic potential, the Board warned. Within a decade, the conventional wisdom had changed and it was commonplace to assert that Britain could not afford to be at the forefront in every area of science.

Notes

1 Report of the Committee of Enquiry into the Organisation of Civil Science, under the chairmanship of Sir Burke Trend (The Trend Report), Cmnd 2171 (HMSO, 1963).
2 Report of the Committee on Higher Education under the chairmanship of Lord Robbins, Cmnd 2154 (HMSO, 1963).
3 C. P. Snow, *The Two Cultures* (CUP, 1959).

4 Stephen Cotgrove, *Technical Education and Social Change* (Allen and Unwin, 1958).
5 Correlli Barnett, *The Audit of War* (Macmillan, 1986) and Martin Wiener, *English Culture and the Decline of the Industrial Spirit 1850–1980* (CUP, 1981).
6 Snow, *Two Cultures*, ch. 3.
7 See, for example, the introduction to Peter Medawar, *Pluto's Republic* (OUP, 1987).
8 Speech by Aubrey Jones M. P. in the House of Commons July 1963.
9 Trend Report, p. 22.
10 Speech by Lord Bowden in the House of Lords, March 1964.
11 *The Economist* 22 August 1964.
12 *The Spectator* 8 November 1963.
13 Speech to Labour Party Conference, 1 October 1963.
14 See, for example, Hilary Rose and Stephen Rose, *Science and Society* (Allen Lane, The Penguin Press, 1969).
15 Keith Pavitt and Michael Worboys, *Science, Technology and the Modern Industrial State* (Butterworths, 1975).
16 'Industrial Research and Development in Government Laboratories: a New Organisation for the Seventies', Ministry of Technology (January 1970).
17 The Future of the Research Council System, Cmnd 4814 (HMSO, 1971).
18 'Selectivity and Concentration in Support of Research', Science Research Council (1970).
19 The Organisation and Management of Government R&D (The Rothschild Report), Cmnd 4814 (HMSO, 1971). The Future of the Research Council System (The Dainton Report), Cmnd 4814 (HMSO, 1971).
20 Review of the Research Councils' Responsibilities for the Biological Sciences, Report of a Committee under the Chairmanship of Mr J. R. S. Morris, Advisory Board for the Research Councils, April 1989.
21 Report of the Machinery of Government Committee under the chairmanship of Viscount Haldane, Cd 9230 (HMSO, 1918).
22 See, for example, 'Science and Public Expenditure 1988', a Report to the Secretary of State for Education and Science from the Advisory Board for the Research Councils.
23 First Report from the Select Committee on Science and Technology Session 1971–72, House of Commons 1972.

24 Sir Herman Bondi, 'What are research councils for?' in *Priorities in Research*, ed. Sir John Kendrew and Jullian Shelley (Excerpta Medica, 1983).

25 Phillip Gummett, *Scientists in Whitehall* (Manchester University Press, 1980).

26 A Framework for Government R&D, Cmnd 7499 (HMSO, 1979).

27 Interview with Sir James Gowans, former Secretary to the Medical Research Council (February, 1989).

28 House of Lords Select Committee on Science and Technology (October 1988); and The Morris Report, 'Review of the Research Councils' Responsibilities'.

29 Michael Shaltock 'Higher education and the research councils', *Minerva* 27, no. 2–3, 1989.

30 Third Report of the Advisory Board for the Research Councils 1976–1978, Cmnd 7467 (HMSO, 1979).

31 Ibid. p. 1.

32 Ibid. p. 16.

33 Ibid. p. 19.

6 Disillusion and Decline: Science in the Thatcher Years, 1979–1990

By the end of the 1970s, the science system in Britain was tottering.[1] In its last plans for public expenditure, the Labour government had promised some respite for basic research: an increase of 1.5 per cent over the years 1978–9 to 1981–2 for the Department of Education's science budget. That, of course fell with the government in the May 1979 election. The advent, at the end of the 1970s, of a Conservative administration more deeply committed than Mr Heath's Conservative government had been at the decade's start to applying the discipline of the marketplace to all areas of national life, meant a further period of uncertainty.

At least three separate strands of policy have become inextricably intertwined in the years of Mrs Thatcher's government. The first was the government's commitment to reining in government expenditure, generating the perception among scientists pursuing curiosity-driven research that their chief sponsor was reluctant to fund their work. In fact, there had been an increase in the science budget, narrowly defined, but the government's rhetoric and real shortages elsewhere contributed to the general perception that funds were lacking. The second aspect of policy was the government's commitment to the marketplace, which generated the perception that 'pure' research was unwanted anyway. The third strand was a consequence of the internal dynamic of science itself: the period of exponential growth in budgets and manpower was over, to be replaced by some sort of 'steady-state' regime, and many scientists found difficulty in adjusting to this regime. Any one of these developments would by itself have produced distress within the community of 'pure' scientists, but all three together produced confusion and despondency.

The greatest confusion has been over just how much public money was being spent on science. The budget for the research councils has actually increased by about a quarter in real terms over the period of Mrs Thatcher's government. However, for university-based researchers, the calculation is complicated by uncertainty over the true distribution of resources from the UGC block grant which represents the second part of the dual-support system for basic research. As a proportion of the national wealth, the resources available through the research councils and the UGC combined have fallen from 0.35 per cent of GDP at the beginning of the decade to 0.3 per cent at the end. This represents a cumulative shortfall of about £1 billion had the 0.35 per cent proportion been maintained throughout the decade. By 1989, the budget was running at about £250 million a year less than would have been the case had the original percentage been maintained.[2]

The government's policy towards science has been characterized by a curious compound of ideology and ignorance. The ignorance was not that of the nature of science itself — regrettable though the fact may be, government ministers of all parties have always been ignorant of basic timescales of research, of how easy it is to destroy a creative team of scientists, and of how difficult and painstaking the effort needed to build up world-class research groups. It appears that, when it first took office, the government was surprisingly ignorant of its own machinery for supporting science: the machinery that had been developed gradually since the First World War. And, at times, there appear even to have been doubts about the fundamental lesson of that war: that modern states have to support scientific research if they are to survive.

Basic science — that research performed for the public good and without the intention of practical application — proved a problem for the incoming government, wedded as it was to the virtues of the market approach to just about everything. The policies of Mrs Thatcher's government are bringing to an end the way basic, curiosity-driven scientific research has been done in Britain for most of this century and, in particular, are dismantling the post-war dispensation and the research system built up in the 1960s, following Sir Burke Trend's reform And yet, the evidence suggests that this change was not intended It was an unhappy accident, accentuated by the trends and pressures that predated the Thatcher administration.

There was a philosophical problem in fitting basic science into the marketplace. Throughout the century, British industry has been reluctant compared to its foreign competitors even to fund applied research; in the 1980s, it had no intention of footing the bill for any work whose immediate application could not be foreseen or whose results could not be protected as intellectual property by patents. In any case, as argued in chapter 2, there is a respectable body of literature to explain that it is not in the interests of any commercial company to finance basic research which its competitors could exploit. Over the decades since the Second World War, basic or pure science has grown steadily more expensive so that it must be supported by the state if it is to be performed at all: the day when a Lord Rayleigh could finance research in his own private laboratory have long since gone. Some areas of basic science notably astronomy and fundamental physics, have grown too expensive even for individual nations to finance by themselves leading to international and intergovernmental projects.

The result has been some confusion, as ministers struggled to understand what science was, and what they wanted to get out of it. The initial reaction was to downgrade the importance of basic, not-for-profit research, and to encourage universities research councils and individual researchers to switch to more applied, or at least applicable, work. However, without prior consultation, in 1988 the government performed a volte-face It decreed that it would not fund 'near-market' research - that was the business of industry, which had been made strong and profitable again after nine years of Mrs Thatcher's government - but that it, the government, was solely in the business of funding basic and strategic research.[4] The policy of the first nine years had encouraged universities and research councils to put emphasis more on applied that on basic research, partly in the hope of obtaining research contract income from administrative departments to supplement the core grant for basic research from the Department of Education and Science. One result of the government's ill-explained switch in policy has been suddenly to deprive research councils of some of this source of contract research income.

The earlier attitude — that research ought to pay its way — was neatly expressed by Kenneth Baker, shortly after he became Education Secretary: scientists, he urged, should experience the delights of the business lunch. There was a certain symbolism also in the change in name of two research councils, to the Science and Engineering Research Council (although this was largely to satisfy the professors of engineering who had been lobbying for their own research council), and the Agricultural and Food Research Council.

When it took office, the government was the inevitable and hapless victim of one of the baleful legacies of Lord Rothschild's dictum that there should be no general oversight of R&D. It was consequently profoundly ignorant of the interdisciplinary nature of science — of how decisions taken by one department of state could affect the scientific interests of others. Even within a single department, that of Education and Science, ministers were apparently unaware that their determination to reduce public expenditure on the universities — the ideological element to the policy — would conflict with their desire to maintain level funding for science. In effect, ministers had not heard of, or did not sufficiently understand, the dual-support system for the funding of basic scientific research.

The money which the Department of Education and Science spends to support basic science is distributed among the five independent statutory bodies who conduct or commission research: the Medical Research Council; the Science and Engineering Research Council; the Natural Environment Research Council; the Agricultural and Food Research Council; and the Economic and Social Research Council. But this science budget which in 1990–1 was £897 million, actually accounts for only a part of the money that the state spends on basic science.[5] In the same year, the Universities Funding Council, the successor to the University Grants Committee (UGC), contributed around £800 million to funding science. The UGC contribution is the second, and historically greater, part of the dual-support system, although the distribution of the money is not transparent. The research component of the block grant is supposed to pay a proportion (around 40 per cent) of the salaries of the tenured staff in universities, all of whom are contracted to engage in research, and this proportion is supposed to represent the time that they devote to research rather than teaching or administration. From this money too comes the wages of researchers' laboratory technicians (who are vital members of a research team in these days of complex sophisticated apparatus). The UGC money also goes to the provision of small items of equipment and 'consumables' – straightforward laboratory chemicals, for example. The UGC contribution was intended to provide a 'well-found laboratory'. Thus, a scientist who had an unorthodox idea that he wished to explore informally to see if it was promising could do so using the facilities of the well-found laboratory funded by the UGC. If the idea did turn out to have promise, the scientist could then apply to the appropriate research council for a project grant to pursue the research further, to purchase large items of capital equipment and perhaps to hire a couple of research assistants. In addition, he or she might take on graduate students to help with the project in the course of their training in research methods. This flexible system is virtually unique to Britain. In this has lain one of the secrets of the productivity and creativity peculiar to British science. It is difficult to find a scientist or scientific administrator who does not believe that the dual-support system was an excellent and a successful way of providing 'risk capital'.

As money has got tighter, it has become increasingly difficult to check up on the distribution of UGC (now UFC) funds to ensure that they are being spent on their avowed purpose. The money allocated to support research is a rather notional quantity the universities get a block grant from the UFC and are expected to spend a given proportion of it on research rather than teaching. If the universities choose to spend it differently, there is no accounting mechanism to track the course of this money. The effect principally of the government's 1981 cut in UGC funding and of other measures has been to cut the state's support of basic science by more than 11 per cent, according to some estimates. Other studies contradict this, and estimate that there has been a rise in government funds for academic and academically related research of between 11 and 15 per cent.[6]

What has happened has been complex. The government decided that universities ought to obtain greater income from fees paid by overseas students and so it reduced the subvention for the UGC to allocate to universities. It appears that the distribution of the money by the UGC, and the autonomous decisions by the universities themselves on how to spend what public funds they had obtained, resulted in a sharp cut in the amount of university money going to science. In effect, university research funds were diverted by the universities to meet other pressing needs. The dual-support system was already under strain in the previous decade, following the collapse of orderly University Grants Committee funding in 1974, and the inexorable trend towards 'big science' exhibited even by what had previously been quite small sciences. But, by the end of the 1980s, the actions of the UGC and of university administrators had come close to breaking it up. Civil servants within the Department of Education and Science recall that 'it came as a surprise to ministers' to learn that their planned UGC cuts could affect science in this way. The confidentiality with which the decision was made – to prevent leaks to the press among other things – meant that the decision process was so compartmentalized that no one was able to gauge the impact until it was too late. Because the distribution of the UGC budget is far from transparent most scientists at the laboratory bench, perceiving only a tightening of funds, have failed to address themselves to the University Grants Committee as the responsible body.

The result was a precipitate decline in morale. For the quarter-century following the end of the Second World War, British university scientists had had access to growing amounts of money, with no strings attached. That changed in the 1970s and the science system was under stress long before Mrs Thatcher's government took office. In the early 1970s, the budget for the research councils fell in real terms. Mrs Shirley Williams, the Secretary of State for Education and Science in the Labour government of 1974–9, confirmed the end of the era of rising budgets with her remark that 'For the scientists the party is over'. Although the budget for the research councils had been rising in real terms since 1980, by 1987 Britain was spending about £300 million a year less on academic and academically related research than its European competitors. To this perceived shortage of cash, Mrs Thatcher's government added an extra strain, by promoting applied research as a desirable end. Scientists who had previously been praised for the excellence and originality of their research, which they believed to be a full-time occupation, now found that they were supposed also to be entrepreneurs, patent agents and miniature industrialists. While these extra burdens were being loaded upon them, they found it increasingly difficult to get funds to carry out their research. Many senior scientists found that they were doing little research but a great deal of form-filling as they applied to various bodies for the money to keep their research teams going.

There was, moreover, an inadvertent and unplanned further stress built in to science funding as a result of the Heath government's decision in 1972 to claw back money from the Department of Education and Science's block grant to the research councils and assign it to other departments for them to commission applied research on the customer–contractor principle. The course of Mrs Thatcher's government and its concern to limit public expenditure has revealed just how vulnerable some of the research councils became under the Rothschild system. The commissioning departments proved careless in their stewardship of the research that it had become their duty to commission. The Agricultural and Food

Research Council, for example, now estimates that its annual income – just over £100 million in 1987–8 – would be some £30 million higher if the Ministry of Agriculture Fisheries and Food had maintained research contracts at a level corresponding to the original amounts withdrawn by Rothschild. Instead, as was almost inevitable, when the Ministry was faced with constraints on its public expenditure, one of the first things to be squeezed was its long-term commitment to the funding of scientific research. A similar situation obtains between the NERC, whose income is also around the £100 million mark, and the Department of the Environment. But the close relationship between customer and contractor had a more subtle effect, particularly on the Agricultural and Food Research Council, whose consequences only became apparent at the close of the 1980s. Whereas the Haldane principle would have allowed AFRC scientist-administrators to identify problems according to scientific criteria, the dependency on MAFF contracts inexorably shifted the balance of the Council's research effort increasingly into the applied science area – precisely the work from which the government has now decided to withdraw funding. The Agricultural Council has therefore suffered something of a double jeopardy over the past two decades.

The Medical Research Council managed to reverse the Rothschild arrangements early in the term of Mrs Thatcher's government and obtained a refund from the health departments of the moneys that had been taken away from it. The council maintains that it welcomes research contract work, but only so long as it is in addition to the core programme of research that the Council's own assessment of scientific priorities indicates to be the correct choice.[8] It is perhaps no surprise that morale among the scientists who obtain funds from the MRC is much higher than that of their peers supported by the other research councils.

So far the discussion has focused mainly on the research councils and academic science rather than publicly funded civil science as a whole. Total public spending on all civil research and development includes UGC money, the budget for the research councils, the research performed in-house or commissioned by other departments, and research grants to industry. It is clear that over the years since Mrs Thatcher took office the government has been devoting proportionately less of the nation's wealth to civil research and development.[9] Spending has fallen from 0.72 per cent of GDP in 1981 to 0.58 per cent in 1987. Had the original proportion of GDP been maintained, nearly £600 million more would have been spent on civil science in 1987. It would take an extra annual expenditure of more than £1 billion to bring public spending on civil research and development up to the same proportion of the UK's GDP as the German government spends as a proportion of its GDP. In absolute terms, the Federal Republic is spending on civil research and development only slightly less than the UK spends on both civil and defence research, so the UK would need to double its civil research spending to match. In proportion to GDP, the governments of Italy, France and Sweden, as well as West Germany, now spend more than does the British government in support of civil science. Of our major international competitors, only the government of the USA spends less than the UK.

In the early years of Mrs Thatcher's government, there was a distinct flavour of government spending public money to make up the deficiencies of private industry. The Department of Trade and Industry's research and development budget actually rose from £138 million in 1979−80 to £323 million in 1983−4, consisting largely of spending in industry to encourage the development of new technology. Most of the 1983−4 budget was actually spent in industry; only about £60 million was spent on in-house work by the DTI's own laboratories. The department was involved in two very significant initiatives to bring industry and the research laboratory closer together. At the beginning of the decade there was considerable fear in the USA and Western Europe regarding Japan's so-called 'fifth-generation' project in computing. Basically, the fear was that the Japanese were about to do for computer programming (which was and remains a British strong point) what they had done in the manufacture of electronic hardware. The talk was of artificial intelligence, of expert systems, of machines that could be programmed in ordinary language or even that would understand spoken speech, of machines that could reason for themselves and that if given the entire knowledge of some expert, a doctor say, could then give more reliable diagnoses than a human. In 1983, the Department of Trade and Industry therefore announced the start of a five-year programme of collaborative research in advanced information technology: the Alvey programme.[10] The aim was to double the research effort in the area. The Alvey programme had five specific objectives: to build up UK expertise in very large-scale integration (VLSI), including a capability to design and make economically 1 micron integrated circuits (presumed to be vital to the new generation of fast compact computers); to create and maintain in the UK tools and methods of producing high-quality software; to build up the country's expertise in intelligent knowledge-based systems; and to increase the country's expertise in man—machine interface, including speech and image processing; and finally to build up infrastructure and communications technology, including the operation of an advanced network to link the information technology community in Britain. The telephone connection to most British houses uses coaxial copper cable — a technology as suitable for the age of computer communications as the pack horse — and the government was planning to replace this with fibre-optic cables that could carry not just telephone, telex and fax messages, but computer data reliably and at high speed, together with cable TV and other interactive services.

To encourage the electronics industry, which has a dismal record of investing in research and development, the government announced that it was willing to match, pound for pound, the spending of companies in information technology research. The benefits have been questionable: cynics have argued that most of the government money went to large electronics companies who then simply cut back on their own in-house research budget because work that they would have done in any case was being subsidized by the state. Because the Alvey programme was not intended to produce tangible marketable products, there are intrinsic difficulties in measuring its success.

In 1988, the Department of Trade and Industry announced that there would be no successor to Alvey. However, the European Economic Community has emerged as a major sponsor of research towards the end of the 1980s and some of the Alvey-related work will be continued as part of a Community programme known as ESPRIT.

Shortly after it decided not to continue with the Alvey programme, the government also abandoned the idea of the optical fibre cabling of Britain.[11] British Telecom is replacing the major networks and other systems which are heavily used with optical fibre cables, but believes that it could cost as much as £20 billion to dig up and replace all the cables to domestic telephone users. As the payback period would be more than 20 years, such work is not an investment that the shareholders of the newly privatized company would favour. British Telecom believes that it might be a profitable investment if it were allowed to transmit cable TV and other services over the optical fibre cables, but the company is prohibited from doing so by the terms under which it was privatized. Britain is not alone in having retreated from this technology; France once had an ambitious *Plan Cable* which has come to nought. But France and other European countries are pressing ahead with a less ambitious technology to allow fast and efficient telecommunications: Integrated Services Digital Network. Britain is lagging several years behind in implementing this system.

The other major initiative, in biotechnology, has been rather more successful, perhaps because biotechnology is relevant to two industries, chemicals and pharmaceuticals, which already have a good record of investing in R&D. Despite this, however, there was concern at the beginning of the decade that the UK was losing out in a technology which might have a market running to £50 billion by the end of the century. A report by Dr Alfred Spinks, the research director of ICI and a member both of ACARD and the ABRC, prompted action.[12] On the research side, the SERC set up a biotechnology directorate to increase the research activity in this area. The AFRC, and to a lesser extent the NERC, also started some biotechnology or genetic engineering projects. One of the more startling products f this research is a flock of genetically engineered sheep, roduced by the AFRC at its Edinburgh Research Station. These animals have had part of the human genetic structure rafted into their own and, as a result, secrete a human protein, lood clotting factor IX, in their milk. By spring 1990, five enerations of these living pharmaceutical factories had been orn and a new company, Pharmaceutical Proteins Ltd, formed o exploit the technique.

On the industrial side, following the establishment in the United States of new biotechnology companies such as Genentech and Cetus, Britain's National Enterprise Board set up a new biotechnology company called Celltech. It has deep links with the research community and looks set to prosper. One of its main product lines makes use of the celebrated monoclonal antibody technique discovered at Cambridge. In its early days, Celltech had the right of first refusal to exploit the research being done by the Medical Research Council. The Agricultural Genetics Company similarly obtained rights over the fruits of research by the Agricultural and Food Research Council. Other start-up companies, many also with close links to research council facilities or with access to the intellectual property rights of research produced at the taxpayers' expense, followed suit. The government had removed the automatic right of the British Technology Group to patent publicly funded research in 1985.

Late in 1989 one of the major shareholders in Celltech announced that it wished to sell its shares. The decision was prompted by the effects of high interest rates and general economic conditions rather than by any doubts about the viability of Celltech itself. The shareholding amounted to more than 30 per cent of the company and Stock Exchange rules require anyone bidding for such a proportion of stock to make a bid for the entire company. The board of Celltech spent months trying to resolve the situation, which raised the possibility that this company, which has capitalized on the intellectual property produced by scientists funded by the taxpayer, might pass into non-British hands.

In 1988, the government let it be known that it would no

longer fund 'near-market' research. The news caused great confusion, not least because no one in any previous discussion of science policy had ever used the term 'near-market' research. A further source of confusion was that the decision was not formally announced at the time: the only written policy statement about 'near-market' research comes in the DTI's 1988 White Paper 'The Department for Enterprise' and refers only to an internal review of the research financed by the DTI itself, a part of which the Alvey programme's successor was killed. But it was not apparent at the time that the DTI's internal review of its research was to be the blueprint for a new government policy for research funded by all departments. The result – confusing to outside observers and to research scientists alike – has been the apparent invention of a category of research solely for the purposes of stopping government funding of it. The logic for the switch in policy came from two complementary decisions. The first was the acceptance by the government that it had indeed to be the chief provider for basic research. The second was that the government should not support work that is properly the responsibility of industry, although government retains a continuing interest in promoting industrial research. There is thus still an element of contradiction in government policy: it believes that companies, not government, know what is in their own best interests, yet government remains anxious that British industry is failing to serve its own best interests in the field of research and development and so is trying to persuade companies to do more. In February 1989 a short report from the House of Lords Select Committee on Science and Technology questioned whether British industry was willing or able to fill the vacuum that will be created by the government's withdrawal from 'near-market' research.[13]

The effects of this apparently sudden policy reversal have been most apparent in the fields of energy research and agricultural research. In 1988, the Department of Energy announced that it would no longer fund anything other than a token programme of research into fast breeder nuclear reactors and that the establishment at Dounreay in Scotland would shut some five years before the end of the design lifetime of the

xisting reactor there.[14] This, together with a decrease in
upport for research into nuclear fusion, leaves a considerable
question-mark over the future of the UK Atomic Energy
Authority, a statutory body set up in the 1950s to provide
advice to government and to conduct research into nuclear
power. The Authority remains the largest single scientific re-
earch organization in Western Europe, but it is now a body of
cientists and engineers without a clearly defined role. In an
attempt to market its research skills, it now trades under the
ubric AEA Technology, but it is having to shed staff in large
numbers.

In the agricultural sector, the effect has been more subtle. At
one time, the hard-pressed AFRC estimated that the decision
would deprive it of £9 million but there will be a much more
severe effect on the Ministry of Agriculture, Fisheries and
Food's own research laboratories. Out of institutional self-
preservation, these appear to be turning to programmes of
work in pure or basic science, work that would be better
carried out in the laboratories of the AFRC. The ambitious
programme on bovine spongiform encephalopathy mentioned
in chapter 2 would appear to be a move in this direction. Two
separate parts of the science system produced two separate
programmes of research on 'mad cow disease'. It is difficult to
see how all the money earmarked for this research can be
fruitfully spent.

British academic science has been creative commercially as
well as intellectually: in a survey of US patents of British
origin, commissioned by the Department of Trade and Industry,
the top ranking patent by far was not granted to a British
company, but resulted from publicly funded research done by
scientists from the Agriculture and Food Research Council
into synthetic pyrethrin insecticides.[15] The second most fre-
quently cited patent was for work on liquid crystals carried out
at Hull University. British industry on the other hand has had
a poor record of investing in research and development. According to Professor Keith Pavitt of Sussex University's Science
Policy Research Unit, since the late 1960s R&D funded by
British companies themselves has grown more slowly than in

most major OECD countries until, by the 1980s, it lagged well behind that of its main competitors. In his contribution to the book *The Evaluation of Scientific Research*, Professor Pavitt warns that this cannot be attributed to an unfavourable economic climate, but to the inability or unwillingness of firms in Britain to commit an increasing share of profits or output to R&D at the same rate as their main foreign competitors.[16] Yet studies have shown a clear correlation between a company's investment in R&D and its economic and market performance.[17] (This is not, of course, a matter of cause and effect. It may well be that a high level of R&D stands as an indicator of other managerial strengths in a company that make it a good performer.)

The post-war trends in British science could not have continued: exponential growth in men and money was clearly unsustainable. But it is arguable that Britain had a lot of catching up to do: that the initiatives of Trend and Robbins could have represented the beginning of a serious and sustained attempt to rectify the deficiencies of decades of neglect in both the training of scientists and in inventing new institutions to finance science as it moved out of the era of the university research laboratory. Yet, there are few signs of policy-makers addressing such questions. Not since the early 1960s has anyone tried to gauge just how many scientists and engineers the country should be producing, nor what proportion of the nation's GDP ought to be spent on scientific research. Instead, the experiment of expansion was abruptly terminated by the ideology of Rothschild and the inflation of the mid-1970s. Scientists in other countries have also had to go through periods of retrenchment, but if they are embarking upon steady-state science, it is at a much higher level than the UK.

The government's restrictions on public expenditure also led to increasing demands for value for money, and raised the question of how the government could gauge whether it was getting value for the money that it spent on research. In administrative terms this led to the establishment of an Office of Science and Technology Assessment within the Cabinet Office in 1986. Its function was to develop evaluation methods, especially for assessing the contribution that government R&D

made 'to the efficiency, competitiveness, and innovative capacity of the British economy'. In a further retreat from Lord Rothschild's system, the Science and Technology Assessment Office also had the task of advising ministers 'collectively' (i.e. through a Cabinet committee on science and technology) on the relative priorities among R&D programmes. The new emphasis on appraisal stimulated a great deal of debate and analysis outside Whitehall on how best to measure the outputs as well as the inputs to government-funded research. The results to date have been mixed at best. Addressing a 1988 Conference on the Evaluation of Scientific Research, the Chairman of the Advisory Board for the Research Councils, Sir David Phillips, warned:

> there is a risk of distorting the whole scientific enterprise so that it satisfies whatever measures we invent ... In all our discussions we return to the issue of counting papers and calculating citation index measures. Do we set about the evaluation of research in this way because there is a very strong light on the numbers of publications and citations, or do these measures reflect accurately what is happening in science and address relevant issues? It seems to me that we neglect many other approaches.[18]

It is much easier to measure the inputs to scientific research than to assess the quality of the output. Money and manpower are easy to count. Little work has been done to try to assess relative national performance in science. The Science Policy Research Unit at Sussex University has been making international comparisons both of the money being spent on basic science and of the scientific papers being produced. The output measures show that a definite decline occurred in the UK's share of world scientific publications during the late 1970s. That appears to have levelled off in the mid-1980s. However, the analysis threw up several anomalies. The recovery seems to have been in applied research and at the expense of basic science and, more worryingly, many subject areas that are important in terms of future technological developments appear to be very weak. Computer science, solid-state physics, metallurgy and polymer chemistry are among those fields of obvious technological and industrial importance where the UK is weak and continuing to deteriorate in world standing.[19]

At the beginning of 1987, a report from the House of Lords Select Committee on Science and Technology gave a pessimistic assessment: 'During the last five years, the general state of science and technology in the United Kingdom has not improved. In some areas it has even become worse. In spite of valiant efforts of individuals to make the present system work, and in spite of a few success stories in branches of science and technology, the overall picture conveys an impression of turmoil and frustration.'[20] Their Lordships went on to warn, 'morale is low in the scientific community. A gap is growing between the potential of science and the resources available to scientists. The academic community is held back from breaking new ground or enthusing its pupils. A brain drain among the best graduates is again evident.'

One of the most public signs of this frustration and turmoil of which the Lords spoke, was the formation, in January 1986, of the Save British Science Society. The formation of such a group of scientists trying to defend basic research in the face of government cut-backs is essentially without precedent in the post-war period. It is only the third such grouping to be formed this century: similar groups came into existence during the other two periods of reform or crisis for science − in the early years of the century, when the necessity for state support of science was being recognized for the first time, and before the Second World War, when the need to reform the system became apparent. In less than three years since its foundation, Save British Science transformed itself, and the government's perception of it, from a body of 'whingeing scientists' to one of the most effective and persuasive groups attempting to influence government policy.

During this period, the government was sending a psychologically negative signal to the research community: it appeared willing to contemplate the UK's withdrawal from CERN, the pan-European laboratory for particle physics in Geneva, which

Britain had helped found in 1954. It is difficult to overstate the psychological impact that such a withdrawal would have had on the whole ethos of basic scientific research in Britain. It would have signalled unmistakably this country's retreat from one of the most important areas of pure science, and one in which the UK had been at the forefront. Indeed, in an article in *New Scientist*, the Nobel Prize-winning physicist, Abdus Salam, maintained that the subject had virtually been founded by British scientists, such as Thomson, Rutherford, Chadwick, Cockcroft, Blackett and Dirac.[21] To have withdrawn would have been to decline to third-rate scientific status. Even to contemplate withdrawal, as the government apparently was doing, was a severe psychological blow. Moreover, the rationale for withdrawal was not clear: all 14 member states of CERN pay a subscription that is calculated in proportion to their national Gross Domestic Product. Thus, proportionately, Britain pays no more to CERN than does Portugal, say. But the subscriptions are calculated in arrears, and they are payable in Swiss francs. Thus, large swings in the value of a nation's currency against the Swiss franc could materially affect the amount to be paid in its own currency.

In the UK, the money for international subscriptions came out of the same 'pot' as the money for science performed domestically: the budget of the Science and Engineering Research Council. The effect of government economic policy in its first couple of years had been to push the exchange rate of the pound high against other major currencies, but it fell quickly thereafter. But as CERN subscriptions were calculated in arrears, the sum to be paid in the mid-1980s – when the pound was at its lowest against the Swiss franc – reflected a calculation based on figures for GDP in 1980–1 when the pound was at its highest. The result was a steady pressure on the Science and Engineering Research Council's budget, limiting the amount that could be spent on science in Britain. But the government refused to compensate the council for the exchange rate movements.

The Advisory Board for the Research Councils and the SERC jointly set up an investigation, under the Nobel Prize-winning scientist Sir John Kendrew, to examine the whole question of Britain's research in particle physics. (Sir John was not himself a specialist in this area of physics). In 1985, the committee recommended that the UK was spending too much on the topic and should cut back (even though the ABRC had in 1979 said that this could not be done) and that the subscription to CERN should be reduced. If Britain could not negotiate a satisfactory deal over its CERN subscription, then the country would have to full out.

In the end, a compromise was reached. The system for calculating subscriptions was revised, and the Italians were induced to contribute more than they had been doing to CERN. (Coincidentally, the Nobel prize-winning Italian physicist, Carlo Rubbia, had just been nominated to succeed to the prestigious post of CERN's Director General; this may have eased the financial pain for Italy). CERN itself set up a review, the Abragam committee, which recommended sweeping changes in the organization's personnel and budgeting policies that should help to keep costs down in future. Despite the final compromise which allowed the UK to remain within CERN, considerable damage to morale had been done.

The indications are that the general loss of morale affecting the country's research scientists has filtered down to prospective students and has affected their choice of university undergraduate course. In the late 1980s, the numbers of students studying humanities, business and finance, and social sciences increased sharply, whereas there was a fall in the numbers taking physical sciences and medicine. Social science undergraduates went up from 34,100 in 1985–6 to 36,100 in 1987–8, an increase of 5.9 per cent. Physical science undergraduates declined in numbers from 20,500 to 19,900, a 2.9 per cent fall. The biggest rise, of 16.1 per cent, was in those studying business and finance: from 9,300 to 10,800.

There have been some changes in government policy. In response to the 1986 House of Lords report, the government announced in 1987 – using the customary coded language – that it was setting up a Cabinet committee on science, chaired by the Prime Minister, and that it was strengthening its advisory committee, now know as the Advisory Council on Science and Technology (ACOST).[22] ACOST meets in secret and it is difficult to assess its effect – it did publish a report advocating development trials for the technology of fibre-optic cabling, but the advice was rejected. The withdrawal from 'near-market' research in 1988 has had some good effect: it was intended that the money released would be redirected towards basic science and this expectation was realized when, early in 1989, the Secretary of State for Education and Science, Mr Kenneth Baker, announced a £300 million increase in the science vote over the following three years, bringing the allocation for 1989–90 to £825 million. The allocation represented a significant shift in policy and meant a 13 per cent uplift in the baseline of the budget for basic science.

The new shape of British science in the universities and the research council institutes is gradually beginning to emerge from this period of painful readjustment. The catalyst was the publication in 1987 of a blueprint for the future of basic science, 'A Strategy for the Science Base'.[23] This document, published by the Advisory Board for the Research Councils, was the first serious attempt to come to terms with the facts of life: a science budget that would at best stay constant in real terms, a scientific establishment that had been conditioned to believe that its income would always grow and that recent history was but a temporary aberration, and a university system in disarray.

The Advisory Board's aim was to encourage scientists to think harder about the management of research in the new era of 'steady-state' budgets. The document envisaged a complete transformation of the British university scene, suggesting that in future there would be three classes of universities: some, designated 'T', would concentrate mostly on teaching undergraduates; others, category 'X', would specialize in a few areas of research and teaching postgraduate students: while only a few universities, class 'R', would be designated as fit to do research over a wide area of science and only these institutions would be funded accordingly. The 'binary divide' in British higher education, the distinction between universities and polytechnics, would also be weakened, as an increasing number of polytechnics undertook research.

In addition, the document presaged a move away from research based in university departments in favour of a research institute system akin in some respects to the West German Max Planck Gesellschaft. The UK role model for such research institutes was the world-famous Laboratory of Molecular Biology at Cambridge, an institute run by the Medical Research Council, which has consistently remained at the forefront of molecular biology since the war. (The double helix structure of DNA, haemoglobin and myoglobin, and monoclonal antibodies are among this laboratory's Nobel Prize-winning successes.) The new mechanism proposed for coping with the increasing expense of science was to set up interdisciplinary research centres. The idea was immediately popular and has remained fashionable. It went through several refinements. At first they were to be inter-university research centres – the idea was that small research groups who did not enjoy up-to-date equipment could obtain the use of better facilities at a different university. But the autonomy of the universities rendered this bold idea for sharing facilities impracticable. The centres are now based each at a single university: they are interdepartmental and intended to raise that university to be a centre of excellence in the given subject. Since there is only a limited amount of money available, the implication (seldom spelt out) is that researchers elsewhere will be deprived of resources. The benefits have been questionable: the first such interdisciplinary research centre, on high-temperature superconductivity at Cambridge University, has not lived up to its promise, and better work is being done elsewhere, despite the funding imbalance. But the basic problem lies not so much with the concept as with the simple fact that restructuring any enterprise costs money, and the administrators of the science system are having to try to restructure basic science without obtaining extra earmarked funds from the government to do so. Thus some IRCs have been looked upon by researchers simply as an easier way of obtaining cash in hard times that will then allow them to carry on in much the same way as before, rather than

s a fundamental innovation in the way that research is to be
one.

Moreover, recognition of the importance of the concept of
RCs was overshadowed by furious reaction to the criticism of
he standards of research at the universities implicit in the
dvisory Board's Strategy document. The explicit proposals
or classifying universities as 'R, T, X' have since been gently
ropped. But the underlying imperative of the analysis remains:
aced with shortage of resources, there must be selectivity and
oncentration of resources on a few centres of excellence.

Although this idea has been most clearly articulated by the
dvisory Board, it has been put into action principally by the
Jniversity Grants Committee (now the Universities Funding
Council) which has conducted two separate but overlapping
xercises in selectivity and concentration of resources — at
east as applied to science performed in the universities. The
verlap between the UGC's two studies has added to the
onfusion that currently surrounds British science policy. In
August 1989, it completed an assessment of the research
trengths of every university in the country.[24] The assessment
s estimated to have taken about 100 man-years of time to
omplete and to have cost something in the region of
4 million. Academic researchers were asked in effect to
ominate what were their two best papers published in the
ve-year period 1983—8 and this 'output' was assessed for
uality in parallel with such measures as the academic's ability
o attract grants from research councils (such grants are awarded
n a peer review system and so incorporate some assessment of
he quality of the research proposal) or from outside bodies.

At the same time as it has been assessing the research
erformance of individual university departments across all
ubjects, the UGC has been reviewing the future of individual
ubjects, such as physics, chemistry and earth sciences, across
ll university departments. The subject reviews took account of
kely student numbers and departmental teaching size — areas
vithin its traditional remit — as well as assessing the research
ecord of individual departments. The subject reviews came
ut unabashed with the philosophy of 'big is beautiful' and

virtually recommended the closure of most of the smaller physics and chemistry departments in the universities. For reasons that are presently unclear, shortly after the subject reviews reported, the UGC abandoned them, using the letters column of *The Independent* newspaper, surely one of the most unlikely vehicles through which to announce a complete reversal of policy, to do so.[25].

The UGC has not abandoned the results of its review of research performance — which also tended to discriminate against small departments — and so there may still be triage among the smaller science departments of the universities. Historically, the business of the UGC has been to provide funds for teaching and 'well-found' laboratories for research — it has never before been in the business of assessing the quality of research (that has always been the remit of the research councils) and, in the view of many observers, it is a task for which the UGC is not properly equipped. Paradoxically, therefore, the UGC has abandoned proposals based mainly on assessing teaching — its traditional remit — while retaining research assessments — which have never been its business. The effect has also been a further diminution of the dual support system, since the UGC explicitly used the research councils' assessment of research projects in its own study.

There have also been signs that the future of the five separate research councils may be in doubt.[26] Much of the work of the Agricultural Research Council overlaps with that of the Environment, while both these councils sponsor work in biology that overlaps with some of the research funded by the Science Research Council. It is possible that Britain may eventually move over to a system of just one National Research Council, a system closer to the US model, which has the National Institutes of Health (the equivalent of our Medical Research Council) and the National Science Foundation (a single research council covering all non-clinical sciences). For the moment however, that idea seems to have been put on ice and a smaller, revamped Advisory Board for the Research Councils, with a full-time chairman, has been established instead.

The story of the Thatcher years has been one of confusion

eading to loss of morale among the scientists. That morale will take a long time to rebuild. In international terms, British science probably stands lower than it did in 1945. The recent past has not been particularly glorious: we have had no recent equivalent of the efflorescence of brilliant talent at the Cavendish Laboratory under Lord Rutherford in the 1930s. It may be that the 1990s equivalent of Crick and Watson, of Perutz and Kendrew, Milstein and Klug, are even now beavering away in some cramped shed in one of our universities, as invisible to us today as those now-great names were in 1945. Yet it is difficult to believe that *fin de siècle* British science holds anything other than decadence.

Nor has the confusion yet been cleared. For nine years, the government urged its scientists to do more applied, commercially orientated work – to contribute to the creation of wealth. Suddenly, and without warning, it changed its mind, without taking care to ensure that industry was ready and willing to fill the vacuum. Pure not-for-profit research is once again what the government says it is willing to pay for. Yet, the UGC's successor, the Universities Funding Council, is slashing and burning its way through the research programmes of university departments without an overall plan or design of how the higher education system will look at the end. It is possible that many smaller universities will lose much of their physics or chemistry research as a result of the UFC action. Large, difficult to manage, and completely unproved interdisciplinary research centres are being set up as scientists scramble desperately for the funds that are available. There is no plan, no overall scheme: above all, there is no confidence for the future. And all the while, our major economic competitors are investing a greater proportion of their national wealth in the support of civil research and development:

Government funding of civil R&D as a percentage of GDP

	1981	1982	1983	1984	1985	1986	1987
Germany	1.05	1.11	1.03	1.00	1.00	0.97	0.96
France	0.81	0.85	0.95	0.97	1.01	0.95	0.91
Sweden	1.01	1.02	1.04	1.03	0.96	0.90	0.89
Italy	0.61	0.61	0.66	0.69	0.70	0.67	0.70
UK	0.72	0.70	0.67	0.66	0.62	0.62	0.58
USA	0.51	0.45	0.41	0.40	0.41	0.39	0.40

Source: Annual Review of Government Funded Research and Development 1989

Notes

1 Parts of this chapter are based on 'The Thatcher Effect in Science', by Tom Wilkie, in *The Thatcher Effect*, ed. Dennis Kavanagh and Anthony Seldon (Clarendon Press, 1989).

2 It is a measure of the ignorance on which policy-makers have based and are continuing to base their decisions about science that these figures have only recently been compiled, as part of a long-term research programme at the Science Policy Research Unit at Sussex University to derive reasonable international comparisons of government spending on civil science. For most of the 1970s and all of the 1980s, there have quite simply been no accurate figures for what is being spent on science. Frustratingly, the figures compiled by the team at SPRU cover 'academic and related research' and bear little relation to the official figures for spending by the research councils or the UFC. See John Irvine, Ben Martin and Phoebe Isard, *Investing in the Future: an International Comparison of Government Funding of Academic and Related Research* (Edward Elgar, 1990). The figures for the decline in basic science funding relative to GDP come from Save British Science, private communication (May, 1990).

3 See Keith Pavitt, What We Know about the Usefulness of Science: the Case for Diversity (DRC Discussion Paper no. 65, Science Policy Research Unit, Sussex University, September 1989) and references therein for a discussion of why industrial companies do not support basic research.

4 As will be noted later in this chapter, there is no formal statement of this radical change in policy, either in the form of a Green

Paper or White Paper. See, however, the speech by the then education secretary, Mr Kenneth Baker, to the Academia Europeana in 1989 for a *post hoc* rationalization of the policy (Department of Education and Science pamphlet, 1989).

5 Annual Review of Government Funded R&D, 1989 (HMSO).

6 The House of Lords Select Committee on Science and Technology was told that there had been an overall 11 per cent decline in funds for basic science (House of Lords, February 1989). Irvine et al., *Investing in the Future*, quote a 15 per cent rise over the period 1980 to 1987. However, because of their definitions of academic and related research, this figure excludes Rothschild-style contract research income. When the decline in that source of money during the 1980s is taken into account, the increase is around 11 per cent. However, their calculations are dominated by 'General University Funds' and if, as is argued in this chapter, some of that money has not actually been spent on its avowed purpose, there is little assurance that the calculation reflects what has really happened to the financial support available to the scientist at the laboratory bench.

7 Irvine et al., *Investing in the Future*.

8 Interview with Sir James Gowans, former Secretary to the Medical Research Council (February 1989).

9 Annual Review of Government Funded R&D, 1989 (HMSO).

10 See Alvey Directorate, Alvey Programme Annual Report, DTI annually from 1984.

11 Mary Fagan, 'Is Britain left behind in the cable race?' *The Independent*, 12 December 1988, p. 17. See also *The Independent*, 4 December 1989, p. 15.

12 Biotechnology: Report of a Joint Working Party of ACARD and Advisory Board for the Research Councils and the Royal Society (The Spinks Report) (HMSO, 1980).

13 Report from the House of Lords Select Committee on Science and Technology (February 1989).

14 Tom Wilkie, 'An energy policy in chaos', *The Independent*, 31 October 1988, p. 17.

15 F. Narin and D. Olivastro, *Identifying Areas of Strength and Excellence in UK Technology* (CHI Research, 1987).

16 Keith Pavitt, 'Technology and its links with science' in *The Evaluation of Scientific Research*, Proceedings of a Ciba Foundation Conference (John Wiley, 1989), p. 50ff.

17 K. Pavitt and P. Patel, 'The elements of British technological

competitiveness', *National Institute Economic Review* 4(122):72–83, 1987.

18 Comments by Sir David Phillips in *The Evaluation of Scientific Research*, Proceedings of a Ciba Foundation Conference (John Wiley, 1989), p. 215.

19 Ben Martin, John Irvine, Francis Narin, Chris Steritt and Kimberly Stevens, 'Recent trends in the output and impact of British science', *Science and Public Policy*, 17, 1 (February 1990).

20 'Civil Research and Development', Report by the House of Lords Select Committee on Science and Technology (HMSO, January 1986).

21 Abdus Salam 'Particle physics: will Britain kill its own creation?' *New Scientist*, 3 January 1985.

22 'Civil Research and Development', Government Response to the First Report of the House of Lords Select Committee on Science and Technology, 1986–87 Session, Cmnd 185 (HMSO, 1987).

23 'A Strategy for the Science Base', Advisory Board for the Research Councils (HMSO, 1987).

24 For a provocative analysis of the UFC's analysis of research quality see Ted Nield, 'A £4 m nonsense to rate university research', *The Independent*, 13 November 1989, p. 17.

25 Letter from Sir Peter Swinnerton-Dyer, *The Independent*, 27 October 1989.

26 Report of the House of Lords Select Committee on Science and Technology (October 1988); and 'Review of the Research Councils' Responsibilities for the Biological Sciences', Report of a Committee under the Chairmanship of Mr R. J. S. Morris, Advisory Board for the Research Councils (April 1989).

7 Conclusion

Britain entered the post-war period still cherishing dreams of an imperial grandeur that had, in reality, already faded. The misperception of Britain's wealth and standing in the world was reflected also in the structure and funding of science. Successive governments spent heavily on prestige projects, such as atomic power and aircraft procurement, without regard for the distortions that this placed on the demand for scarce skilled scientific manpower. Successive governments also continued the practice of funding scientists in the universities and elsewhere without asking whether the work they were doing would yield any commensurate economic benefit to the country.

Throughout the post-war period no one has doubted that there was a connection between science and economic development. Were science merely a cultural activity, it would have been funded at much lower levels than has historically been the case. But there is little agreement on, indeed there has been little analysis of, the mechanisms that connect science, innovation and industrial development. Consequently, there is little guidance as to how much money it is prudent and reasonable to invest in science. In Britain towards the end of the 1980s, the government was devoting 0.58 per cent of the nation's GDP to civil research and development, whereas it had been spending 0.72 per cent of GDP at the beginning of the decade. Both figures are arbitrary, yet no one throughout the post-war period has been able to suggest what proportion of the national wealth it would be rational to spend on civil research and development.

Science has its own internal dynamic: at any one time, the amount of science to be done is at least proportional to the stock of knowledge, so as our knowledge of the natural world grows, science grows still faster. But national wealth does not grow at the same pace, and whereas for much of the post-war period science consumed an increasing proportion of the country's GDP, there had to be a limit to growth. The un-answered question, as noted above, is precisely where it is rational to draw that limit. Most of Britain's serious industrial competitors appear to draw it more generously than British governments (regardless of political party). The story of science in the second part of the post-war period has been one of reluctant and grudging adjustment to the realities of budgets and a shortfall of cash compared to the scientific opportunities opening up. This collision between the expanding frontier of science and cash limits has been most publicized in the area of basic research funded by the state, but such limits exist also in industrial research and put an even higher premium on com-panies' ability to pick winners.

The period after the Second World War was one of rapid expansion of research laboratories at universities and central large research facilities, with all the consequent problems and growing pains. However, some sciences had changed qualitat-ively, rendering university-scale laboratories inadequate. The Manhattan Project symbolized this change: in just a few years, physics had changed from being the sort of thing to be pursued in the basement of the old Cavendish building, to being a major industrial project employing thousands of staff at major sites across the whole of the USA. Subsequently, other sciences have followed physics into the realm of what is now known as 'big science'.

As some sciences took on this quasi-industrial character, the requirement inevitably grew that they should be properly managed. But the way in which the state had channelled its support to basic science in Britain militated against this: indepen-dent statutory research councils were interposed between the individual scientist and the political paymaster, to allow researchers almost untrammelled freedom to pursue whatever research they found interesting. There was no one to manage the allocation of expensive research facilities in the overall national interest, nor was there anyone to suggest that basic science ought to have a closer connection with the industrial and commercial world. The decisions in the 1950s that the Cavendish Laboratory would not continue its long established line of research into the fundamental constituents of matter and that the new national particle accelerator, Nimrod, should be located near the Atomic Energy Authority's Harwell site, taken together with the poor technical performance of that machine when complete, seem today like errors of judgement. But there was no mechanism by which the Cavendish could have been nominated as a national centre of excellence in particle physics. Nor, even by the 1970s, were the consequences of establishing large research institutes properly mastered, as exemplified by the reluctance in the mid-1970s to shut the Rutherford Laboratory when Nimrod had reached the end of its usefulness. As the post-war period progressed, even what have traditionally been small sciences have started to enter the big league. Chemistry laboratories, if they are to be state of the art in terms of chemical analytic technology, require gas-chromatography/mass-spectrometers costing in excess of a quarter of a million pounds each. A well-equipped solid-state physics laboratory might perhaps wish to enjoy the benefit of a molecular beam epitaxy machine at a cost of more than a million. The announcement of an international programme to map the entire human genetic blueprint, the human genome project, is perhaps the most recent example of 'bigness', this time in molecular biology.

The managerial question of science is, if anything, more acute today. The problem is that in the 1950s there was a willingness on the part of successive governments to spend money on science, which could have facilitated the resolution of the problem; whereas in the 1990s, there is a marked reluctance to spend on science. Closing research institutes that have outlived their usefulness is expensive in terms of redundancy payments if nothing else, but little extra money has been granted by government in recent times to cover such 'restructuring' costs. The administrators, primarily the Advisory Board for the Research Councils, are having to make bricks without straw and, because no one agrees on what shape the building should be anyway, bits of it are always been pulled down only to be rebuilt.

There seems to be little effort devoted to recognizing the present and easily predictable future problems that will confront British science. Scientists with permanent jobs in the universities are getting old. There was a massive intake in the late 1950s and early 1960s, and there will be correspondingly large numbers retiring from the mid-1990s, without a new generation coming up to succeed them. As things stand, much research in British universities is currently being done by a shadowy army of research assistants who live a hand-to-mouth existence on a succession of short-term contracts. The very existence of these post-doctoral research assistants is something of a mystery. Their numbers have apparently doubled over the 15 years to 1990, yet the money available from research council grants to support them has not increased by anything like that proportion. Has the science system attempted to continue exponential growth despite budgetary constraints, by hiring cheap labour in the form of these research assistants? If so, where is the money coming from? What happens to these highly qualified people when they reach the end of their three- or five-year contracts — do they go abroad for better conditions and more security, thus contributing to a brain-drain of young talent? If this is the case, it is a brain-drain that is completely unremarked and un-monitored because of the impermanent status of the research assistants.

The equipment with which scientists in the universities are expected to do their research is obsolescent. It may be that some of the money that would have been spent on equipment has been diverted to pay the salaries of the research assistants just discussed. Pressures have built up over nearly 20 years, since the end of exponential growth in the science budget, and will need both flexibility and new money to solve. Both are in short supply.

On the industrial side, some of the more obvious distortions in the patterns of government spending on research and development have been corrected in the 1980s: funding on aircraft and on nuclear power has at last been reined in. But the diversion of scientific talent and money to economically unproductive defence research has not been tackled. It remains the case that chemicals and pharmaceuticals are Britain's leading science-based industries, with a good track record of investment in research and development and of export and financial performance. It is perhaps significant that neither industry has any connection with defence. The British record in electronics, telecommunications, and computers — the other great science-based industries of the post-war era — is much patchier, even though a great deal of money has been spent on research in this era. The suspicion must be that much of the effort has been misdirected into defence-related work that had little civil spin-off. Britain has no domestic manufacturer of television sets, nor any indigenous mass-producer of consumer electronics; the country's flagship manufacturer of mainframe computers, ICL, was absorbed by STC in 1984 and its modern computers now use chips made by Fujitsu, a Japanese manufacturer which, in 1990, bought ICL itself; nor does the UK have any major manufacturer of personal computers; Plessey, an innovative electronics company, has been taken over partly by GEC and partly by Siemens of West Germany. British designers have produced new computer chips: the Inmos transputer, Active Memory Technology's Distributed Array Processor, the Acorn ARM chip; yet it is foreign companies that appear to be taking the lead in exploiting these designs or it is in foreign markets that such products are better received.

In the late 1980s, Mrs Thatcher's government had the courage of its market-orientated convictions and announced that 'near-market' research and development would not be funded by government. Such research was the proper business of industry, in the government's view. The decision marks a break with the tradition of decades of government subsidizing industrial research in the hope of encouraging companies to innovate and compete in high-technology and high value-added products.

Yet even Mrs Thatcher's government could not quite shake off the feeling that British industry was not to be completely trusted to act in its own interest. The government still believes that it has a role in promoting the benefits of research to industry and there are still schemes, such as the LINK initiative, where the state will match pound for pound the investment of industry in specific research topics. In 1988, together with 18 major companies, the government also took a leading role in setting up the Centre for the Exploitation of Science and Technology which is supposed to bring the benefits of British science to the attention of British industry. More than 70 years after the first research associations were set up to encourage British industry to make more use of the fruits of science, it is difficult to avoid the conclusion that little has changed.

The purpose of this book is to survey what has happened in British science since the war, not to propose policy nor look to the future. Inevitably, the story does not have a neat conclusion and there are many loose ends. Are the universities still the right institutions in which to conduct basic scientific research? The Advisory Board for the Research Councils' discussion document, 'A Strategy for the Science Base', hinted that they may no longer be adequate in these days of interdisciplinary research using expensive equipment beyond the means of any one institution. Many of the universities set up in the Robbins expansion have remained comparatively small in terms of student numbers, staff and finances. Often they have larger institutes nearby, called polytechnics, fulfilling very similar functions. There is a logical case for amalgamation; the continuing binary divide between universities and polytechnics is a very considerable anomaly. Polytechnics are now producing more than half the graduates at first degree level in Britain and, in some fields, the quality of research being done in polytechnics is better than that in some universities. It is a measure of the institutional rigidity of this country that such a possibility is not even a topic for debate, let alone action. One suspects that the response from the university sector would echo the view put forward by Oxford and Cambridge universities after the war: that any change would be for the worse and would lower standards. T regenerate the morale of British scientists, it might be worth going back to the proposals put forward at the end of the war. Is it worth resurrecting the idea that Britain should set up Institutes of Science and Technology to rival MIT and Caltech?

Is the diffuse and decentralized system, whereby individual government departments operate their own laboratories and commission research out of their own budgets still appropriate? The continuing friction between the Ministry of Agriculture and the Agricultural Research Council suggests that it may not be. Is it worth bringing all the government's research laboratories together under one organization, as was proposed at the end of the 1960s? The sheer lack of knowledge of what is actually going on within the science base (as exemplified by the research assistant phenomenon or the opacity with which UFC funds are distributed) indicates that a more coherent system of monitoring the fate of taxpayers' money is called for.

But it is the relationship between science and industry that leaves the most unanswered questions. All governments have been preoccupied with trying to get British industry to exploit science, with comparatively little success. Even Mrs Thatcher's government, as has been observed, could not quite find the courage to step back and declare that, in this area, business knows best. The experiment of Mintech was abandoned at the end of the 1960s; are new mechanisms required to encourage the exploitation of science? France, Germany, and to some extent Japan, have powerful government departments to over-see not only the funding of pure and applied science but also its take-up by industry, but there is no political impetus for such change in Britain.

There have been many calls in recent years for a Minister for Science once more to be established, but none of the proponents have been able to solve the problems that defeated Lord Hailsham's busload of civil servants in the late 1950s and put forward a scheme where the minister would have real power in Whitehall, industry and among the scientists. Yet, as the European Community becomes ever more important both in the industrial sector, and as a sponsor of scientific research, Britain is at a continuing disadvantage in terms of its representation on the council of ministers and the various subcommittees. When science and technology are discussed, France and Germany are represented by their science ministers, who are significant political figures domestically also. Britain is represented by a junior minister from the Department of Trade and Industry, while basic science (which it is government policy now to support) remains unrepresented because domestically it lies within the Department of Education and Science. The future of the Department of Trade and Industry is itself under review. Once it has been divested of purely regulatory functions, what sort of rump will remain? Could it be that the 1990s will see the reconstitution of a Department of Scientific and Industrial Research, to which are answerable not only the existing research councils, and the government's own laboratories, but also an Industrial Research and Development Authority?

With the advent of the single European market in 1992, those who have advanced scientific skills can vote with their feet. At around the same time, demographic changes mean that fewer young people will be entering the university system and subsequently employment, so there will be increasing competition for graduate manpower from all sectors of industry, further reducing the numbers who will pursue careers in science. In the mid-decade also, a large tranche of university scientists who embarked on academic careers at the time of the great Robbins expansion will be coming up for retirement and there are few experienced younger staff in post ready to replace them. There will be a similar development in the United States, perhaps prompting US academic recruiters to cast their nets in the UK.

Against this background, unless there are radical changes, the UK apparently intends to try to compete in the international marketplace for high-technology goods, while its science has been marginalized politically, fragmented administratively and largely ignored industrially. The prospect is not inspiring.

Appendix: Definitions of Research and Development

In 1981, the OECD succeeded in agreeing a consistent set of definitions of research and development, published in what has become known as the Frascati Manual, *The Measurement of Scientific and Technical Activities*.

According to the Frascati Manual, research and experimental development (R&D) comprise creative work undertaken on a systematic basis in order to increase the stock of knowledge, including knowledge of man, culture and society, and the use of this stock of knowledge to devise new applications. Research and development is a term covering three activities: basic research, applied research and experimental development.

Basic research is experimental or theoretical work undertaken primarily to acquire new knowledge of the underlying foundation of phenomena and observable facts, without any particular application or use in view.

Applied research is also undertaken to acquire new knowledge. It is, however, directed primarily towards a specific practical aim or objective.

Experimental development is systematic work drawing on existing knowledge gained from research and practical experience that is directed to producing new materials, products or devices, to installing new processes or to improving substantially those already produced or installed.

However, the British government has altered the definitions to suit its own purposes and incorporate the concept of 'strategic research'. This required broadening the Frascati definition of applied research to include 'work towards practical aims which cannot be identified'. How anyone can work towards an aim that they cannot identify is mercifully left unclear. Strategic research thus becomes 'applied research which is in a subject area which has not yet advanced to the stage where eventual application can be clearly specified'. Non-strategic applied research is expected to have quite specific and detailed products, process and systems as its aims. At this point the definitions tend to acquire the arcane character of the medieval theological debate about angels dancing on pin-heads. For, having accepted albeit a modified version of the Frascati definitions, the Annual Reviews of Government Funded R&D provide quite different criteria for the funding of science. These purposes are:

The advancement of science: This is equivalent to the Frascati term basic research, with the rider that 'although originally funded with no specific application in view, much of it eventually results in long-term benefit through the eventual application of knowledge gained'.

Support for policy formulation and implementation: Applied research and experimental development carried out to meet the government's own needs for knowledge or improved products or processes. An example might be research to clarify what policy and choices the government should make with regard to renewable energy sources.

Improvement of technology: Applied R&D, funded by government departments but often carried out in industry to advance the technology of different sectors of the UK economy.

Support for procurement decisions: Applied R&D which contributes to the specification and development of goods and services required by departments and to equip the purchasing department to be an informed buyer. This category is mainly related to defence needs.

Support for statutory duties: Applied R&D which assists departments to discharge their statutory obligations under, for example the Health and Safety at Work Act or the building regulations

Support for the humanities: This category is necessary mainly to accommodate the peculiarity of the English-speaking world which tends not to classify social science in the same category as the natural sciences.

Other activities: Applied R&D that does not come under other headings, for example, research to support agricultural progress in developing countries.

Two further categories of government spending on science and technology have been introduced recently. They do not come within the Frascati definitions of R&D, but are included under the science and technology rubric in the government's annual statements on public expenditure:

Technology transfer: The prime objective of this activity is to encourage the exploitation of knowledge in a place different from its origin.

Restructuring costs: This includes redundancy awards for the closing of research institutes or transferring their functions elsewhere.

Chronology

1913   Medical Research Committee, forerunner of the Medical Research Council, set up under the terms of the 1911 National Health Insurance Act.

1915   Formation of a Committee of the Privy Council on Scientific and Industrial Research.

1916   Establishment of the Department of Scientific and Industrial Research.

1918   Publication of the Haldane Report on the Machinery of Government, which set out the principle that government ministers should not control or direct research.

1919   Establishment of the University Grants Committee.

1920   Memorandum by Christopher Addison, Minister for Health, on the Medical Research Council, providing the clearest articulation of the 'Haldane principle'. Medical Research Council created by Royal Charter.

1931   Agricultural Research Council created by Royal Charter.

1946   Report of the Barlow Committee on Scientific Manpower, advocating a doubling of the numbers of scientists being trained in universities.

1947   Advisory Council on Scientific Policy established to oversee the administration of civil science. Defence Research Policy Committee established to cover military research.

1948   Development of Inventions Act which set up the National Research Development Corporation.

1949   Nature Conservancy created by Royal Charter.

951 Return of Conservative government under Winston Churchill. Tizard resigns from chairmanship of both ACSP and DRPC. Sir John Cockcroft appointed chairman of DRPC and Alexander Todd chairman of ACSP.

952 Imperial College raised to university rank, in partial fulfilment of Barlow Committee recommendations.

954 Atomic Energy Act sets up the UK Atomic Energy Authority.

955 Committee of Enquiry into the Department of Scientific and Industrial Research, chaired by Sir Harry Jephcott.

956 Department of Scientific and Industrial Research reconstituted by statute.

957 National Institute for Research in Nuclear Science created.

958 NIRNS granted its own Royal Charter.

959 Lord Hailsham appointed Minister for Science.

962 Committee of Enquiry into the Organization of Civil Science appointed under the chairmanship of Sir Burke Trend.

964 Publication of Trend Committee report. Labour Party wins General Election. Harold Wilson becomes Prime Minister.

965 Science and Technology Act. Science Research Council, Natural Environment Research Council and Social Science Research Council created by Royal Charter. Ministry of Technology established. Council for Scientific Policy formed to advise Department of Education and Science. Advisory Council on Technology formed to serve Ministry of Technology.

966 Central Advisory Council for Science and Technology formed to advise Cabinet Office.

967 Ministry of Aviation subsumed within Ministry of Technology.

968 Formation of International Computers Ltd (ICL) as a result of Ministry of Technology's intervention in the British computer industry.

970 Conservative government of Edward Heath elected to office.

1970 Civil Service Department suggests that Ministry of Agriculture, Fisheries and Food should take direct control of the Agricultural Research Council.

1971 Publication of Dainton Report on 'The Future of the Research Council System'. Publication of Rothschild Report on 'The Organization and Management of Government R&D.

1972 Advisory Board for the Research Councils established to advise Secretary of State for Education and Science.

1972 Nature Conservancy Council separated from the Natural Environment Research Council.

1974 Labour government elected.

1976 Formation of the Advisory Council for Applied Research and Development.

1979 Conservative government under Margaret Thatcher elected.

1980 Publication of the Spinks Report on biotechnology.

1981 Department of Health agrees to return 'Rothschild money' to Medical Research Council.

1983 Launch of the Alvey programme of research in advanced information technology.

1983 Agricultural Research Council becomes the Agricultural and Food Research Council and the Social Science Research Council becomes the Economic and Social Research Council.

1985 National Research Development Corporation merged with the National Enterprise Board to form British Technology Group and loses its right of first refusal to patent publicly funded research.

1986 Save British Science movement founded to oppose cutbacks in state funding for basic science.

1987 Advisory Council for Applied Research and Development is replaced by Advisory Council for Science and Technology.

1987 Publication of 'A Strategy for the Science Base' by the Advisory Board for the Research Councils.

1988 Department of Trade and Industry White Paper announces that government will no longer fund 'near-market' research but will concentrate on basic and strategic science. Massive reductions in fast breeder reactor research programme announced. Government decides that there will be no successor to the Alvey programme.

989   University Grants Committee is replaced by Universities Funding Council.

Index